When People Pray

AN OMF BOOK

© OVERSEAS MISSIONARY FELLOWSHIP
(formerly China Inland Mission)
Published by Overseas Missionary Fellowship (IHQ) Ltd.,
2 Cluny Road, Singapore 1025,
Republic of Singapore

First published 1987

OMF BOOKS are distributed by
OMF, 404 South Church Street,
  Robesonia, Pa 19551, USA
OMF, Belmont, The Vine,
  Sevenoaks, Kent, TN13 3TZ, UK
OMF, PO Box 177, Kew East,
  Victoria 3102, Australia
and other OMF offices.

ISBN 9971-972-58-1

Printed in Singapore

Contents

Denis Lane, OMF's Director for Home Ministries, has
written the introduction to several books in this series.

*When
People
Pray*

THESE DAYS we like things to work. Brought up
in a scientific age that explains everything from the
secrets of DNA to the size of the universe, we are
impatient with things that don't work. The first
question we tend to ask about some new idea is
"Does it work?" So we naturally ask the same
question about prayer. Does it work?

This book is not an attempt to answer that
question, because it is the wrong one to ask.

Our scientific western culture thinks automati-
cally in terms of cause and effect. Without these
rules science could not have discovered anything.
So we want to apply them to everything, including
prayer. But prayer is a mystery, and you cannot
analyze a mystery. Mysteries may frustrate us, but
they are a part of life, indeed the richest part of life.

The book of Proverbs tells us that one of four
things the writer could not understand was "a man
and a woman falling in love" (Prov 30: 19 GNB).
Physiologists can describe the chemical reactions

that take place when someone falls in love, psychologists can explain some of the behavioural symptoms, and sociologists may talk about the part this relationship plays in the continuity of the human race. But none of them can begin to explain or even describe the mystical magical glory of the man/woman relationship. That defies analysis. So it is with prayer.

Prayer fascinates us. Books on prayer sell readily. Yet prayer meetings in most churches are poorly attended, and missionary prayer meetings are usually left to the elderly. Can it be that we have tried to analyze and categorize prayer into a manageable science, and then turned away in despair when it defies our attempts to contain it?

This book tells us some of the things that have happened when people have prayed. As you read it you will soon discover that there is no automatic relationship between a prayer and its answer. To think that I can pray tonight and have the answer infallibly by the morning is clearly wrong.

What in fact does happen when people pray? One of the simplest and clearest descriptions ever given is this: "Prayer is to let Jesus into our needs. To pray is to give Jesus permission to employ His powers in the alleviation of our distress. To pray is to let Jesus glorify His Name in the midst of our needs."

The missionaries who wrote these chapters have done that, and in doing so have found Jesus near

O. Hallesby, *Prayer*, IVP

and His grace sufficient. When Adam and Eve chose their own way in the garden, the Lord shut the door to the garden, and Adam and Eve shut the door to their own hearts. Since then man has been self-sufficient, confident of his ability to know and choose the difference between good and evil, and quite capable of managing his own affairs. Prayer is simply the reversal of that process.

In prayer we allow God into our lives, and expose ourselves to His working. We open the door, and let Him in. That is why prayer is impossible for the sinner unreconciled to God. How can he expose himself to God and give Him access to a life that is determined to go its own way? You have to be careful these days whom you allow through your front door. Strangers may have come to assault and rob you. So you secure your front door with bolts and chains. When God is the visitor and allowed even to put His foot in the front door, who knows what may happen? Prayer can be a dangerous business.

Prayer is expressing our dependence on God for His wisdom to know what we ought to do and to have the strength to do it. The common concept of prayer is twisting the arm of the gods to do what we want. But Christian prayer confesses our ignorance and asks for direction as to what we should do. In the Garden of Gethsemane, Peter thought he had all the answers to any attempt to arrest Jesus, and therefore needed sleep more than prayer (Matt. 26:36-46). Jesus understood the issues and wrestled before God to conform His will to His Father's.

Christian prayer needs no qualifications except a sense of weakness and dependence.

Prayer is exposing our circumstances to God and His sovereign purposes. When James was killed by Herod, and Peter was spending his last night on earth in Herod's prison, the church was praying (Acts 12). We are not told whether they were praying for Peter's release, for his strengthening, or for their own reactions to this seeming disaster. They simply knew their weakness and Herod's political power. The answer surprised them. When Rhoda forgot to open the door to the freed Peter because she was so happy, the praying group could only give a spiritual explanation: it must be his angel. Perhaps they did not realize at the time that for Peter to have died then would have thrown in question all his activities in preaching the gospel to the Gentile Cornelius. That in turn could have restricted the expansion of the gospel in all the world. So the Lord set him free. Because the church had prayed, they could have a part in this drama, and share in God's sovereign purposes.

Prayer is a means of communion. Because prayer is letting God into our circumstances and our lives, we need to listen as well as to speak. Our generation is obsessed more by communication than communion. We are a talking generation, but find it hard to listen. Virginia Stem Owens pointedly writes, "Has no one noticed that communication is a matter of sound and communion one of silence?"[2]

Communion becomes the instrument for receiv-

[2]"The Total Image" (Eerdmans 1980)

ing direction. Communion with God rebuilds the spiritual tissues of the soul as food and sleep restore the tissues of the body. You cannot describe the results of communion in terms of concrete effects. A husband and wife who spend a quiet evening together may not be able to tell you precisely what that evening accomplished. Were they wasting their time?

The people who have written in this book do not profess to be experts. They are simply human beings who know their weakness, and in that weakness have allowed God into their lives and circumstances. They do not see magnificent miracles every day of their lives. Nor did the apostles. Apart from Paul and Silas in Philippi, we do not read of anyone else delivered from prison in answer to prayer. Peter himself, and later Paul, both suffered martyrdom uninterrupted by the angels. Nor were they lacking in faith. They simply walked in the freedom of the presence of God and His sovereign purposes, allowing Him to direct them and trusting Him to strengthen them. Through prayer they had learned to walk humbly with their God.

We live in a world of Oscars, astronauts and Superman. If you are not super-something, you are nothing. Yet the early church was made up of slaves and servants, the humble poor, the ordinary people. God is looking for people who are weak enough and simple enough to allow Him into their lives and circumstances. Omnipotence plus weakness equals strength. When people pray, God works.

Bob Trelogan, *from UK and originally a vet, has been church planting in Thailand for more than ten years.*

Innocent in Prison

PRASIT'S CASUAL ELECTRICIAN'S JOB took him to remote villages to lay cable. How he hated the squalid environment of gambling and girls in the workers camp. To get home to his wife and baby was expensive and inconvenient but he tried to when possible, even though missing the last bus after dusk meant walking a few kilometres. Camp was often in the local temple, and when Prasit had to stay overnight he'd sit and read his Bible until night fell. His workmates commented on his high standards.

The electricity board office stood just across the road from a petrol station. The station owner called the police to report that, two days before, three youths on a motorbike had held her at gun point and stolen 2000 baht (US$90). The police arrested her unemployed neighbour and the man in his home with him who was an electricity board employee. They then gave her photographs of all the electricity board employees, and she picked out

Prasit as the third robber. When the police arrived to arrest him at his work camp, he was surprised. But he submitted to the indignity of leg chains, knowing the mistake would soon be discovered.

When he returned from army training, Prasit had thrown his initiative and enthusiasm into the weak and insecure church at Phayuha. He became its first and only elder. My wife Jan and I relaxed a little and went off happily to Faith Academy in the Philippines, to see how its secondary system would suit our Scottish teens. Ernest Ng from Hong Kong, the third member of the Phayuha missionary team, met us at the airport on our return with the bombshell sentence: "Prasit is in prison, charged with armed robbery."

We were disappointed and upset, of course. But we were sure victory would be just round the corner. Hadn't we seen God work just before we left for the Philippines? In answer to prayer a threatened marriage breakup was defused and a pregnant teenager situation alleviated. We'd had the joy of seeing confession and reconciliation. *Okay. Now to pray this through too. God must quickly release an innocent man. Especially Prasit, His gift to Phayuha church.*

Prasit's months in Uthaithani jail weren't pleasant, but he had plenty of cause for optimism. The three accused pleaded not guilty, and everyone saw clearly that they didn't know each other. The prison governor commented on Prasit's obvious innocence, and offered to find him an able lawyer. The public prosecutor assured them of justice.

There was talk of suing for damages after winning the case, and calling in the anti-corruption squad. Prasit's mother gladly paid 15,000 baht (US$675) to get the legal procedures started satisfactorily.

Christians from four different churches visited Prasit and a friendly warder made sure medicine, literature and other gifts reached him. Prasit witnessed faithfully. One man believed and two others gathered for Bible study and daily devotions. Permission was given for a large Easter service and handing out of tracts. After each month's court hearing Christians prayed and claimed justice and truth.

Prasit was worried about his wife and child. He'd already made it tough for them by refusing to pay the bribe to release himself from military service. He had soldiered the full two years while Duan supported herself selling noodles. Could her faith stand this further test? With a baby as well, the financial situation was nearly hopeless.

Gradually, as news of Prasit's imprisonment became known, Central Thailand churches and missionaries and then Christians overseas sent in material support. "It's as if God pays my wage," Duan said. Jan was concerned that she'd doubt God but instead she steadied up spiritually and emotionally and began sharing her faith in the little Sunday School.

Bail was granted to Prasit the very day we flew to Scotland for furlough! That and the petrol station owner's contradictory statements filled us with hope that the ordeal was over.

The morning of the final trial, the Central Thailand missionaries were spending the day together at the conference centre. After praying they waited expectantly for Ernest to arrive from court with the good news. He arrived, but with a white face. The three men had been found guilty and given the maximum sentence of eighteen years. They were to be transferred to the top security prison for murderers and gangsters at Ayuthya. All the evidence had counted for nothing against an untruthful woman's word.

Life was suddenly much harsher for Prasit, and his faith plummeted to rock bottom. Numbly looking at his Bible, he gradually began to realize that David's experiences in the psalms were just like his own. The plight of Israel in the book of Isaiah was helpful too. Prasit belonged to the same God!

The feeble light of his faith flickered, then burnt brightly again. He started to witness to the variety of hardline criminals around him — Muslims, Buddhists, animists, hardened sceptics. He had long, tough dialogues with men who openly showed their enmity to this Christian.

All through the first year Prasit cried to the Lord over and over again to save him from destruction both physical and moral. He was saved from a brutal gang war, the assailants armed with metal bars, because he obeyed God's prompting to go and talk things over with one of the attackers. Around him was filth, homosexuality, murder and revenge. But he concentrated on the positives — crafts for a small income, haircutting, arbitrating even for his enemies. These enemies became good friends when they saw how Prasit helped them when they were in trouble.

During the second year he became aware how his letters both to Phayuha church as a whole and to individuals were bringing blessing. Three more men believed and were nurtured in the Christian faith. Then the younger brother of one of Prasit's chief enemies was converted in Bangkok. This opponent heard of his brother's dramatically changed lifestyle and approached Prasit, asking, "What is this power that changes the lives of people as awful as my brother?" Prison warders gave permission for a big Christmas party with games, prizes, balloons, and a tract for each prisoner.

Prasit's first and second appeals were rejected. So when the third and final appeal was to be made to the Supreme Court, all prayed with even greater determination for his release. Through letters we heard of increased prayer around the world. Through our children, other children heard and started to pray with great seriousness and discipline.

During his two years in the army Prasit had worshipped at a church in Bangkok. This church now offered to pay his legal fees and supply one of their members as a lawyer. The lawyer didn't give much cause for hope. Being a new graduate, he hardly made the essential "Who's Who" group at Supreme Court level. He also warned that because the backlog of cases was so great, the end of 1987 was the likely appeal date. Others said that often the Supreme Court increases rather than decreases sentences, but with good behaviour he might perhaps be released after five more years.

By this time two other Christians were being held in Uthaithani jail, unjustly accused of murder, their case equally hopeless. They and Prasit corresponded with each other, encouraging each other in the God of Hope. The situation stimulated Thai Christians to stand more strongly for truth and justice, and claim victory in the Name and for the sake of the Lord Jesus Christ. Duan insisted on coming with us to the first trial of these Uthaithani Christians. "I want to encourage them to stand firm for Jesus too," she said, as she moved her toddler from one hip to the other.

Six days after the Uthai murder trial, Duan was watching TV in her neighbour's house. The neighbour scoffed at trusting a God who didn't act. "Why doesn't He release your husband?"

"Oh, He will soon," Duan replied. A few nights before she had dreamed they were together again. She was sure God had given her that dream. She was sure God had said September 5th, too, but hesitated to speak of it to others.

On the same day, in Ayuthya, Prasit and the other two men convicted of the robbery were called to the prison governor. He read to them a letter stating that their appeal had been heard in a special session of the Supreme Court in Bangkok and was successful! There was no evidence against them. They were free!

Prasit gave his clothing and meagre belongings

away, except for his Bible, books and guitar. He checked his money — just enough for the bus fare home and no more! He looked so rough in shorts and torn T-shirt, with open infected sores all over his legs, that the driver wasn't interested in stopping the bus for him on the highway near the Phayuha intersection. Prasit had to use prison tactics and threaten to jump off. It was after dark on September 5th, 1986.

I had been out all day on September 5th, and returned wearily at 7.30 in the evening. Was I seeing things? There was Prasit, with his child on his knee and Duan close by, sitting and talking with Jan. Weariness changed to wonder and joy as we heard how God had suddenly and effectively vindicated His servant. It was the one solution that had been beyond our most imaginative hopes. We had been praying towards a royal pardon on the auspicious occasion of the King's sixtieth birthday, on December 5th, 1987, fifteen months away. God had answered far more abundantly than we had even thought, much less asked. Prasit was completely cleared of any guilt, and all without buying the help of any influential person!

Phayuha never lost its church elder. A lady in the church received a picture of his being trained in prison, like Joseph, for a leadership ministry. Prasit sees it in the same way. He worked rapidly through higher level Bible correspondence courses, challenged and encouraged Phayuha Christians by mail, and emerged a more refined and respected leader than ever before. He and I are coworkers now that Ernest has moved to another town!

Dr Diana Dunn's *husband Michael is in charge of OMF work in Indonesia.*

The Ins
and Outs
of God's Plans

NICOLA FELL ILL on the last Monday of her Christmas visit home to Indonesia, where we are working at OMF's headquarters in Jakarta. Her older sister had returned to England the previous day in a tropical downpour and we had all got wet as we saw her off. Nicola and her brother, Adrian, were due to fly back the following Sunday in company with another girl, Mary.

For supper that Monday night, Nicola had chosen to have noodles. We had just started preparing them when she complained of a tummy-ache and took herself to bed.

Oh dear, I thought. *Maybe Nic won't want much supper after all.* She didn't. She was running a fever, which went up ... and up ... and up.

Being a doctor is a mixed blessing at such times. Concern for a sick daughter is mixed with clinical cares: What's causing this fever? Did she get chilled at the airport last night? Could this be malaria — in spite of taking anti-malarial tablets faithfully? Is it going to develop into something serious? I did not know any doctor conveniently near whom I wanted to consult, so I looked after her myself, examining her once or twice every day for signs to indicate the cause of the illness. Apart from fever and lack of appetite, there was nothing. A blood test showed nothing out of the ordinary, either. By the third day the fever was over 40°C (104°F). Mercifully Nicola did not seem as ill as you might expect. But she was worried that she might not be fit to travel back to England on Sunday with Adrian and Mary.

"I don't want to have to fly back to England by myself," she said. "And if I'm late back to school I shall have tons of work to make up." She prayed fervently every day that God would make her well again in time to fly back as planned. We prayed too, confident that our heavenly Father delights to hear and answer children's prayers: confident that He knows what is best for us. Towards the end of the third day the fever began to subside and her nose started to run like a tap. She used up tissues by the boxful. By the Friday the fever had almost gone, but had left Nicola pretty weak. Was she making progress fast enough to be fit to travel? Would it be fair on two fourteen-year-olds on the long flight, which included changing planes in Singapore? Would it be wise to expose a young girl to such an endurance test when barely recovered?

Our doubts tugged on the one side, her pleading on the other. By the Friday evening I was convinced we could not take the risk of letting her travel in such a weakened state. We should cancel her seat on the plane. She would have to go back later ...

Then an idea popped into my mind. I could take her home myself! That way, it would be less critical how strong she felt for the journey as I could help her. I could see her into school when she was ready, and meet her housemistress and Adrian's housemaster, neither of whom I had met before.

My excitement grew as the possibilities developed in my mind's eye. While in England, I could go and see my aged mother, who had moved into her own room in an old folk's residential home, with all her chosen things around her. My heart leaped at the thought! For months I had longed to go and see her, for she was in her ninetieth year and evidently failing fast. How I should love to see her again and encourage her in the Lord, if possible. But I had received no indication from the Lord that I should leave my work to do so. Was this the opening I longed for? When I suggested it to Michael, my husband, he agreed. The Lord had been leading us along identical paths of thought.

Early next morning we phoned the airline office to enquire about bookings for the following Friday. Yes! They had places for us. So we made the bookings and cancelled Nicola's seat on Sunday's flight. Then we went to break the news to her. She was disappointed, asking why God hadn't answered her prayer. In her heart of hearts she knew the decision was wise, for she did not feel strong enough to travel yet. But going back to school late ... all the extra work ...

"Why didn't God answer my prayer, Dad?" Her piercing question was not easy to answer. We don't know all the ins and outs of God's plans.

Michael replied the only way he could:

"I don't know why God has allowed you to be ill just now; but He must have some reason, which maybe we shall understand later on."

We had an eventful time during the five days Nicola stayed home with us after Adrian and Mary had flown back to England. On the Monday night it rained and rained and RAINED. Solid, unrelenting, tropical downpour. We woke up in the night as the sound penetrated the quiet drone of the air conditioner. Michael got up and went out onto the verandah to check the level of water in the yard. He came back to bed for half an hour, but next time he looked out the water was higher and would soon be into the house and offices.

He went round the Mission Home rousing adult residents. "Everybody up! All hands on deck!"

When Michael went downstairs he met a small army of cockroaches fleeing into the offices under the front door, in advance of the floodwaters. We went to work to save as much as possible from the flood, lifting books from bottom shelves and emptying bottom drawers of filing cabinets. Everything which would spoil was lifted onto tables or carried up to the first floor verandah. Someone went round disconnecting all electric appliances from flood-level sockets.

Having started in good time, we did not suffer any damage to speak of. Just mess! But the front wall of the yard next door collapsed under the weight of water and damaged the junction box, cutting off our telephone. No outside calls could be made, nor incoming calls received. (Someone was heard to remark on the blissful peace!)

When Nicola and I flew off to England on the Friday evening, three days after the flood, the phone was still cut off. I had instructions to phone OMF International Headquarters from the airport in Singapore to give them another number in case they needed to contact us urgently. The phone was answered by one of the senior ladies, whom I knew well. After I had given her the message, she said, "Your sister phoned here last night, trying to contact you. She seemed to think you might be here."

My sister? She knew very well I was due to fly to England this Friday. Why would she want to phone?

"Did she leave any message?" I asked.

"No, she didn't."

"OK then. Thank you. Bye."

That's very queer, I thought. *Very strange indeed.* My family is not given to phoning blithely round the world to pass the time of day. If there were any question about the hire car she was arranging for me, surely she would wait until I arrived. *My mother! What about her? Had she been taken ill? Had she ...?*

I hurried through the airport after Nicola, who was being taken in a wheelchair as she was too weak to walk far. One aftermath of the flood had been a tummy bug which hit several of us, including Nicola, knocking the stuffing out of her again.

As we had left the OMF Mission Home in Jakarta, the Indonesian office staff had gathered round and prayed for our journey. Our heavenly Father has interesting ways of answering prayer. Scheduled to take sixteen hours, the journey took over 28! Fog closed Abu Dhabi airport so we landed in Dubai instead. Then fog descended on Dubai and we could not leave. A row of jumbos were lined up on the tarmac and the terminal building was swarming with transit passengers. We were thankful to find seats.

The long wait at Dubai proved a resting period for Nicola. Meanwhile, I had time to meditate on the news I had heard in Singapore. Considering its import, I was surprised by my own peace of heart. Wasn't I desperately disappointed if my mother had died just before I could see her again? God's Word assured me, "Our times are in His hands." If this was the way a sovereign heavenly Father had planned it, so be it. But, maybe she was still alive after all, only very ill ... However, the family had not phoned on previous occasions when my mother's health had given cause for alarm.

My conviction remained steady that I was flying home to share in my family's time of loss. We had not planned that. Before I left England last time, my sisters had agreed that I need not come home for such an eventuality. Evidently God planned it otherwise. Sitting in an aeroplane, even a big, stable jumbo jet, one has a sense of flying through the air ... of course! Perhaps for that reason Deuteronomy 33: 26-27a came to my mind:

> "There is none like God, O Jeshuran,
> who rides through the heavens to your help,
> and in his majesty through the skies.
> The eternal God is your dwelling place
> and underneath are the everlasting arms."

Physically we had been flying through the air. Almost as tangibly I could feel those divine arms bearing me up and carrying me to England to be on hand to take part in the funeral service, to share with my sisters in the bereavement and to help deal with the business matters.

My sister, who met us at the airport twelve hours late, was taken aback to see a wraithlike Nicola being pushed along in a wheelchair. She was also surprised at the calmness with which I received the confirmation of my suspicions.

"Did you get the radio message I sent from Dubai, warning you we were delayed by fog?" I asked.

"Yes, I did, thank you. Did you get the telegram I sent you?"

"No, I didn't. We had a flood and the telephone was cut off."

"Ah, that explains it. We tried to phone you for two days. The operator assured us the queer note we got instead of the ringing tone was normal for international calls! It was only when we asked another operator that we learned your phone was out of order, so we sent a telegram."

That was enough. We were not more explicit. Nicola did not know what we were talking about, and I did not want to break bad news to her in that situation.

I learned later that the telegram reached the OMF office on the Saturday morning, twelve hours after we had left and three days after it had reached Jakarta. For once, I was thankful for the delay. It would have been very distressing to receive such news just before leaving home. "Our times are in His hands" even down to tiny details.

I could not share with my sister the overwhelming sense of God's presence in all that long journey home. But Nicola realized that God had been hearing her prayers after all, and she understood that He had answered them according to His divine Wisdom.

Barbara Griffiths, *nee Good, is from New Zealand and has worked with the Hmong tribe in North Thailand for 20 years, most of the time with Barbara Hey (see page 27).*

Rats! ... God's answer?

I ARRIVED puffing and panting in the Hmong village after two to three hours walking through the teak forest and up the steep hills. All the Theological Education by Extension (TEE) students were home, and we sat around the church leader's kitchen table for several hours in the afternoon and evening and had a good study on Luke's Gospel. In typical Hmong fashion I was invited to eat the evening meal in several homes — fortunately one can eat just a little in each place!

My coworker Barbara Hey was home on furlough. Apart from the huge job of preparing TEE materials and trying to keep one step ahead of the students, I also had to visit five villages in five different provinces each month to discuss with the students what they had been studying.

The day before I had set off from our home in Rock Village, with new TEE study books to give the students, and enough money in my purse to cover the whole journey. After a walk, a bus ride and a night stopover in the Chiang Rai mission home, I took another bus before my long walk.

The next day when it came time to leave, the church leader's wife and several others tied huge sacks of peppers on to their backs and accompanied me to the road. They could have gone any day to sell in Ngao, but decided to come with me so I would not have to walk alone. Their bus north came first, and soon afterwards my southbound bus also arrived. I hopped on, and got out my purse to pay the fare. It was only then I discovered that most of my money was missing. Once I'd paid the fare there was scarcely any left.

I sat stewing over it. I had enough money to get to New Yellow Creek, but that was all. What should I do? My mind started chewing over possibilities ... *Should I ask the Hmong when I get there? ... Surely if I tell dear old Noah he will lend me some?...Maybe the Lord will remind people to pay those medical bills that are still owing from when we used to live in New Yellow Creek?...And goodness, what will I do for food?* In New Yellow Creek we still had our own house where we always fended for ourselves, instead of staying with the Hmong as we did in other villages.

I'm embarrassed to ask the Hmong for food or money. It doesn't seem quite like following our faith principles of moving men through God by prayer alone...How can I hope that the Hmong will follow those principles if I don't follow them myself? ... "Oh Lord, please will you supply my food needs at New Yellow Creek, and my money needs for fares for the rest of this trip. Lord, I'm trusting you. You have promised to supply our needs."

So ran my thoughts over and over many times on the three to four hour journey to Tak. Sometimes I would rest in trust in the Lord, and at other times I would take the burden back on my own shoulders and worry.

On reaching Tak I went to the open market and bought a cabbage, which left me with just enough for the fare to New Yellow Creek. I had hardly been in our house in New Yellow Creek ten minutes when in walked Mrs Noah with a gift of meat (they had killed a wild deer) and a big bunch of bananas. I had some rice in the house so now I was well set up for weekend meals. I thanked Mrs Noah and thanked the Lord in my heart. *How soon will it be before the Lord reminds some of the Hmong that they owe medical money?* I wondered. Then I felt that maybe I was telling the Lord how He should answer my need, so I again committed the whole matter to Him to answer as He saw fit.

The afternoon wore on busily, with people coming in one after the other to chat. I was several times tempted to mention my need, especially when those who owed me medical money popped in. In the evening there was the church prayer meeting with plenty of visitors before and after. By the time I went to bed I still didn't have a penny for the next part of the trip, and I was starting to worry again as I tucked my mosquito net around me and wondered how it could possibly be so hot at 10 pm. I again asked the Lord to meet my need, and told Him I wouldn't ask the Hmong but was trusting Him to supply my need.

The next day, Sunday, was one of those days when one never stops. After the church service early in the morning I spent a few hours with the TEE students and chatting with people. By 2.30 pm I had not had a moment alone since breakfast and hadn't even had time to make my lunch. I was tired, and was finding it a battle to wait for the Lord to answer my need. After all, I was leaving at six am the next morning and I still didn't have any money. Usually someone would remember a medical bill and pay it, but not this time.

At that moment, just when the last visitor left and I thought I could cook my lunch, in walked Lau, a lovely Christian teenage girl. "Teacher," she said, "we've run out of Sunday school teaching materials. Could we have some more before you go?"

Oh no, I thought. *They surely haven't run out yet. Barbara left them enough for longer than this. Oh Lord, this is too much. Do I have to get more Sunday school things ready this afternoon as well as more TEE work, and also finish preparing for teaching at the church service tonight? Oh Lord, it's too much...and I haven't had any lunch yet.* I told Lau I'd get something ready. By three pm she went off, and I had lunch and again committed my way to the Lord and asked His forgiveness for my negative thoughts.

After eating I had half an hour to spare before seeing the TEE students, so I began looking to see if we had any Sunday school materials packed away in our tin box. That would save staying up half the night to prepare them. There were none in the tin box, and my heart sank, but then I thought of Barb's desk drawer. I knew she'd left a few things there when she went on furlough.

I pulled open the drawer and there before my eyes was one huge mess. The drawer had become a rat's nest, with mother rat and five babies staring at me. Mother disappeared in a flash, and I took the babies out and fed them to the cat. Then I sat on the floor with the drawer beside me and looked at the mess. I could have cried.

"Oh Lord, it's not fair," I told Him. "This is too much! There's so much to do today and now I have to clear this up,...and Lord, I still don't have any money to go on to the next village tomorrow. Oh Lord, please help me...forgive me for not trusting you or resting in you."

Every bit of paper in the drawer had become rat's nest, and I began scooping it out and putting it in the rubbish basket, but carefully in case I needed to write to Barb and tell her that anything special had been ruined. Everything had been chewed to mincemeat to make the nest, except for one envelope halfway down in the back left-hand corner. I nearly threw it straight in the rubbish basket, knowing that rats carry such things as hepatitis. But suddenly, thinking I'd better check it was empty, I pulled it open. Inside were two one-hundred-baht notes — enough for all the rest of the trip!

Right there on the floor beside the drawer and

the rubbish basket I praised and thanked the Lord, and confessed my bad attitudes. He had provided in His own special way and in His own time. I never knew that one day I would be thanking the Lord for rats! When I wrote to Barb about this incident, she replied that she had no recollection of ever putting 200 baht in her drawer.

My heart was light for the rest of the day. At the end of the evening service Noah suggested to everyone that we have a time of testimony, and I shared with them all how the Lord had met my need and taught me more of His love and care. The amusing sequel was that late that evening and very early the next morning several people came to pay their medical bills! God in His goodness supplied even more than I needed.

Barbara Hey *is also from New Zealand. See previous chapter.*

Met — by divine arrangement

"TIME FOR THE RADIO." Day after day for thirty minutes in the early dawn, the small bamboo and thatch hut tucked high in the mountains of north-west Thailand filled with the sound of Hmong Christian songs and teaching. Radios in the other four or five houses nestled on the same small slope tuned in to the government-sponsored Hmong language half-hour, but Mr Four was more interested in the message from Far East Broadcasting Corporation, Manila. From the first time his accidental fiddling with the knobs had brought the Good News to this wee corner of Maehongson province, Mr Four's heart had been gripped by the truth he heard.

One day, after talking it over with his two wives, Mr Four came to a big decision: his family would believe in Jesus. But how did one do that? Using what knowledge he had of how to write in the Thai language, he composed a letter requesting help to burn the things used in his demon worship and turn to the Jesus way. "... and it's easy to get here," his letter continued. "Just follow the trail that leads off the end of the runway at Maehongson airport. You can't go wrong."

Where to send the letter? Surely there must be "Jesus people" in Chiang Mai, the biggest city of North Thailand. So the envelope was simply addressed "To the believers in Jesus, Chiang Mai," and the post office mail sorter dropped it into Box 27. The OMFer who collected the mail was intrigued by this unusually-addressed envelope. "Ah, it's from a Blue Hmong. Give it to the two Barbaras."

We added the name of Mr Four and family to our prayer list — but what could we do about helping him "burn"? The nearest Christians to him were Mr Gar-Boh's family, almost a hundred kilometers south. They had been steady believers for three to four years — perhaps one of them would go.

We sent word off to the Gar-Boh family, and they chose the eldest son, Mr Ring. Mr Ring was willing to go but wanted a companion and preferably a missionary one, so journeying the eighty kilometers to Maehongson he sought out the OMF missionaries to the Shan people, whom he already knew. Don Wilson agreed to accompany him.

The trail off the end of the Maehongson runway became a long, l-o-n-g trail awinding, up and up and UP. Aware of every aching muscle in his perspiring body, Don marvelled that Mr Ring always knew which of the forks in the trail to follow.

That evening after the simple rice meal was over

Don, completely exhausted, lay down to rest. As he drifted in and out of sleep he rejoiced to hear Mr Ring explaining to the Four family what it meant to be a Christian. And within Hmong culture, too! Finally Mr Ring and the Four family took down the spirit shelf, collected other bits and pieces around the house connected with the spirit way, and burned them. Then the family prayed and committed themselves to Jesus.

Next evening, as Don relaxed his stiff, tired limbs while telling his wife Martha all that had happened, he couldn't help being a little thankful that Mr Four was a Blue Hmong and not a Shan new believer. He felt for us who would have to visit Long Climb!

A few months later we planned a trip to visit Blue Hmong Christians in four villages scattered along or off the Chiang Mai – Maehongson Road. We were well aware of the need to go on further and visit Long Climb to encourage the Four family in their new faith. Mr Four had told Mr Ring and Don that he'd like the Blue Hmong-speaking missionaries to visit, and to bring some books and tapes. So we collected together a literacy primer, Bible, hymnbooks and one of the small cassette players we loan to Christians, with at least ten tapes of singing and teaching, and stuffed them into our rucksacks along with our own books, sleeping-bag, change of clothes and so on.

As we set off one thought niggled: it was obvious from what Don had told us that Mr Four's "can't-go-wrong" trail was all too easily go-

wrongable to the non-Hmong-reared Barbaras!
"Lord, we do feel it's necessary to go to Long
Climb," we prayed. "If that's right for us and the
Fours at this time, please give us a guide — or at
least someone who can explain the trail well enough
for us to go alone."

Late in the afternoon, two nights before we
planned to go to Long Climb, we reached Huai
Yuak, three hours' ride south of Maehongson. Thai
passengers in the big orange bus eyed us curiously
as we prepared to alight in the middle of nowhere.
Clinging to the down-side of the winding, tree-
shaded road were three or four teak-leaf-roofed
houses. As usual a warm, "You've come, have
you?" welcomed us to the homes of these believers.

In the course of the usual conversation about
such important things as fields, crops and health
came the question "... and where are you going to
from here?" Barb and I exchanged a hope-filled
glance. For some reason we had understood that in
the end it was Mr Par from Huai Yuak who had
gone to help the Four family "burn".

"Well, Mr Par, we really want to go to Long
Climb to visit the Four family — you know them,
don't you? We don't think we can find the way
alone. You wouldn't by any chance be free to take
us, would you?"

Mr Par beamed cheerily at us. "Oh yes, I could
go with you. I'm not too busy with field work just
now." Then he added as a sort of irrelevant
afterthought, "I've never actually been up to Long
Climb before."

In hope-deflating surprise we looked back at him. "But wasn't it you who went to help Mr Four burn his spirit things?"

Mr Par shook his round head. "No, it wasn't me. It was Mr Ring from Mae-ong-khong. But I'm happy to go with you tomorrow." After further discussion Mr Par finally decided that after all he would not accompany us. "Never mind," we said encouragingly. "If God wants us to get to Long Climb He'll certainly make it possible somehow." Brave words, but my heart at least was not quite so assured!

Late next morning, as we waved goodbye to the Huai Yuak folks from another big orange bus headed north for Maehongson, we were still wondering how the Lord could work things to get us to Long Climb. Tonight we were to stay with Don and Martha in a Shan village eight kilometers out of Maehongson town. Maybe, just maybe, Don would go with us? But we knew how completely exhausted he'd been on the trip with Mr Ring!

After several days of speaking Hmong and eating rice meals it was pleasant to chat in English over a foreign-style supper. "... And what are you doing about getting to Long Climb?" Don and Martha asked, knowing we planned to visit there on this trip.

As we explained how our hopes of Mr Par taking us had been dashed, we were surreptitiously watching Don's face. We could read his inner struggle. *I've been. I know the way. I ought to offer to take them — but, oh no, it's such a gruelling climb*. But Christ in His gentleman won as Don said, "Well, I could take you."

We demurred. "Well, I could at least take you about halfway," he changed his offer, "to where you couldn't go wrong on your own." We were thankful for this possibility — but still we demurred. "Let's pray about it," we concluded. So the four of us very simply committed the next day into God's hands. Later, as I fell asleep, I had peaceful trust that God really *did* have it in His control, including having mercy on Don — probably! I couldn't dismiss the offer of "halfway" altogether!

The next morning after breakfast we two Barbaras sardined into the converted pick-up buslet that runs between the village and Maehongson. Our plan was to see if we could find any Hmong in the market who could give us instructions about the Long Climb trail. The chances were slim. Many days there were no Hmong to be seen in the market! Don rode his motorbike in, wondering, *Will I have to go part way? Please Lord, let there be Hmong who can help them!*

Alighting from the buslet at the crossroads in the centre of town, I looked around me. On the diagonally opposite corner my eyes almost instantly registered the navy-blue, knife-pleated, brightly-embroidered-band skirt of a Blue Hmong woman. Excitedly I turned to Barb clambering off the buslet beside me.

"Barb, look, there's a Blue Hmong lady. Your language is better than mine, go and ask her if she knows anything about Mr Four and how to get to their village." Somewhat diffidently Barb crossed the street, and I lugged our packs along behind her. As Barb framed her question, her eyes took in the man standing in the open-fronted shop behind his wife, busily writing a letter. "Excuse me, do you know a man called Mr Four of the Jung clan who lives at Long Climb?"

Suddenly, before the lady could utter a word, the man turned. A beaming smile broke over his face. "Yes, that's me. You must be Nsay and Mblah."

Enthusiastically each side told the other of how God had led us to meet. Mr Four explained, "We only got to town yesterday and are about to go home today. We'd planned to come the day before but one of the children was sick. He's okay though. He's home with my second wife." Then he explained, "I've just been writing to you two to ask you to visit and bring me some books, a cassette player and tapes. I'm anxious to learn all about the Jesus way and I want to become literate in Hmong."

We grinned at him and pointed to our rucksacks. "You can screw that letter up. We've got all those things here for you now."

Don came over from parking his bike and smiled delightedly as he recognized Mr and Mrs Four. "What a wonderful answer to prayer. What a relief not to have to make that climb again!" Thankfully he returned home to share the story with Martha.

My heart sang with thanks the rest of that day too: as I watched the Fours cook "brunch" at the Thai home they'd stayed in the night before; as I strolled along behind them on the stream-bordered path beyond the airfield (and to my eyes "can't-go-wrong" was far from true!); as I puffed and panted up and up and up the stony trail; as I admired miniature Maehongson from high in the woods; as I enjoyed the Creator's touch in the pretty little wild flowers tucked in the grasses by the path winding along the sides of the lightly forested hills; as in the twilight I clambered down the rocky defile that preceded the final "up" to the wee village; as finally I sat, worn out, in the Fours' tiny bamboo shack. Yes, God was good. He had answered prayer all round. "Thank you Lord. We met — by Your divine arrangement."

Mary Teegardin *is now retired in the USA after a lifetime of missionary work in China and Thailand.*

I'll never be a missionary again!

SHORTLY AFTER the Communist takeover in China, two first-term missionaries from different countries and backgrounds found themselves living together in a large provincial city on the banks of the Yangzi River in the far west. The more senior workers had already had to leave because of ill health. I was the younger of the two junior workers, still experiencing many of the "growing pains" of a new missionary.

God had clearly called me and led me to China. Of that I was confident. I knew He would supply all my needs. But in true "knowledge," that is the "knowing" which comes only through experience, I was an utter novice.

A year had passed since the new conquerors had come to our region. One by one, restricting regulations had limited our normal missionary outreach. We could no longer visit daughter churches in the surrounding rural areas, or share in the weekly Sunday School classes at the city church and children's meetings in a nearby soap factory, owned by one of the church elders. Open-air meetings formerly held in the city, and the nightly preaching in the street chapel at the front of the mission compound, were forbidden. Attendance at the regular church services dwindled, because church members had to attend conflicting government-sponsored meetings scheduled for the same hours. Finally, a request to convert the now-unused church and classrooms into government housing could not be refused. Trips outside the mission compound walls, whether for exercise or for shopping in the local food market, had been strictly limited. Friends who formerly dropped in to chat no longer came because of fear, long hours of work, and programmed activities.

God was limiting. Yes, it was truly God who was limiting our outreach ministry, because of the unlimited ministry He proposed to do in my heart.

My fellow worker and I shared a bed in the back section of an old earthen-floored Sunday School room. A large literature cupboard partitioned the bedroom from our dining-living area where we also received official callers. We had spaded the tiny lawn outside our room and seeded it with vegetables, partly for diversion, but hopefully also as a source of food while we waited for our exit permits. The general evacuation order had come from our mission headquarters at the coast, but government permission to leave our station was delayed.

As we waited for our permits, the winter cold that seeped through our paper windows and up from the damp floor gave way to the warmth and beauty of spring. However, small irritations arose from the frequent harassments and questioning by different authorities, and grew into big ones.

As I sought to stifle my turbulent reactions to these situations, my heart grew bitter. I questioned the ways of God. Why was I still here? Why couldn't I have been somewhere else, with someone else? I did cry to Him; but my cries arose out of a stubborn and rebellious heart, not a surrendered one.

The days and nights of waiting continued; two, three, four, five months passed. The petty irritations multiplied, until one day I was reported to the Production Board for picking string beans from my garden before they were fully mature — thereby wilfully being wasteful of China's productive soil. The accusation had been made by a neighbor billeted in one of the rooms of our mission home, whose children I had seen picking beans from our bushes a few days earlier. It seemed more than I could bear!

As the days of waiting grew longer, I became ill, unable to eat or keep liquids down. Finally, a Chinese doctor was called, and his medicine helped.

The Lord had a purpose in those days of distressing illness. He spoke to me, and I saw clearly the rebelliousness of my heart. I began to pray — really pray. I asked Him to forgive my sinful, questioning heart and my undisciplined spirit. I thanked Him sincerely for all the circumstances that surrounded me there, and told Him that I was willing to stay right there, with the fellow worker He had given me, for as long as He knew I needed that learning experience. I grew stronger, and some days later I was asked to assist in a neighborhood inoculation campaign. Now we could leave the confines of our tiny room, and God had opened again a small door of ministry.

What I did not know then was that at the very time of my illness, perhaps the very day of my repentant prayer, my home church back in the United States had felt constrained to hold an all-night prayer vigil asking for my release from China. Three weeks later, exit permit in hand, I was steaming down the Yangzi River toward freedom and home.

Back in that little room in China I once vowed that if I ever got away from there I'd never be a missionary again. How glad I am that the Lord did not hold me to that foolish vow! In His mercy and love He allowed me another 34 years in Asia to watch Him answer innumerable prayers for His glory.

Elizabeth Otten, *from Holland, works in South Thailand.*

It can't be true ... can it?

AS THE TRAIN hurtled through the night I was feeling a bit anxious. I was on my way from Amsterdam to Lausanne in Switzerland. Whole families would come on board loaded with skis, going for winter sports holidays. I was travelling by myself, to attend my first ever Christian conference. And it wasn't going to be a small one! Three thousand young people from all over Europe were expected in Lausanne for Mission '76. I was a bit scared. *Will I be lost in the masses?* I wondered.

I had prayed that God would give me some friends during the five-day conference between Christmas and New Year's Day. But, looking round me in the compartment, I suspected that the other passengers weren't heading for the conference but rather for the white snowcapped mountains of Switzerland. I prayed again, "Please Lord, give me some friends during those days, for I'd hate to feel lost and lonely." Then I turned on my side and went to sleep. Hopefully the next day would bring some friends.

The following day, after changing trains, I realized that most of the other young people were travelling in twos and threes. I envied them, as I hadn't been able to strike up a worthwhile conversation with anybody yet. At last we came to Lausanne.

As we got off the train I chatted with some girls and a fellow and joined them. We had to wait a while before we could register, and got to know each other a little. After registration we walked together to the military barracks which would be our dorm. We girls went together and arranged a place to meet Fritz later. All through the conference we stayed together as a foursome, going our own ways at times but usually having our meals together. Ten years have passed since then. Suzanne has gone to South Africa and I to Thailand, but we still keep in touch a few times a year. The Lord surely gave me friends during that conference!

I had many questions in my mind during Mission '76, and I was praying that God would clearly lead me. Should I be going out as a missionary with a denominational mission, as my pastor had suggested, or with the faith mission with which I had come into contact, the Overseas Missionary Fellowship? Being a nurse, would I have to go to a Bible college? My pastor didn't think it necessary as I would be working in my own profession. And if I did go, which Bible college would I choose out of the bewilderingly long list?

Every morning we had devotions together in

small groups. One of the members of my group was a pastor, and I decided to chat with him about the choice of mission. Being an outsider, he wouldn't necessarily sway me one way or another.

As we talked together it became clear to me that through the OMF God had made me aware of "mission", whereas I hadn't had anything to do with the denominational mission so far. Since God had used them it seemed that He was leading me in their direction. So in due course I went to the OMF stand and established a link with them.

Besides the main meetings we could choose out of many seminars, and one afternoon a seminar was held for medical people. "Please, Lord," I prayed, "make it clear to me in this lecture whether or not I should get a Bible college training, and if so at which college?"

The seminar was held in a large lecture room with people spread out all over the place. Two speakers, one French and one English, gave informative and challenging addresses, and then there was time for questions. I had two burning questions to ask but I didn't dare to ask them. I was sitting in the middle of a row, so it would mean walking to the end of it and asking the questions into the microphone and, to make it worse, not even in my mother tongue! Despite my burning questions I stayed put, I couldn't muster up courage. But God knew how I was feeling, and a girl at the end of my row got up and asked the same two questions! Through that seminar I knew that I had to go to Bible college, even though I would go out to the mission field as a nurse.

One of the speakers that day was Mr Martin Goldsmith from All Nations Christian College in England. To me those names didn't mean anything. Not knowing much about the OMF I wondered if they had their own Bible college, or worked with one particular one. When I asked them about it, they mentioned All Nations Christian College. Since it was through a lecturer of that college that God confirmed to me that I had to go to Bible college, I saw God's hand in leading me and applied to study there. Two and a half years later I entered All Nations and God finalized His answer to my prayers.

At that seminar, I felt *so* thankful to God and to that girl who had asked "my" questions. So afterwards I went over and told her how grateful I was. I discovered that her name was Linda and she came from England. She worked as a physiotherapist in a small London hospital called Mildmay Mission Hospital. We exchanged addresses, and eight months later I found myself working in that same hospital as an auxiliary nurse while I was waiting to get my English nurse's registration. I was living in another hospital.

As I read my Bible one morning during those days I came across the words: "All things work together for good to those who love God and are called according to his purpose" (Rom. 8:28). My heart cried out: *It's not true, it can't be true, and if it is I'd like to see it!* I did love God, but I couldn't believe this verse.

That very day my best friend was coming from Holland to visit me, and she would be staying for a few nights. Up till then it had been possible to have a friend stay in a guest room, but just the day before I had heard that it was no longer allowed. I couldn't have her stay in my own room as that was forbidden because of fire regulations. In our part of London there wouldn't be any accommodation available, and besides, she was coming this very morning and I had no time left to arrange anything. Even if we could find accommodation in another part of London, we would waste a lot of time travelling to and fro.

How is God going to answer? What kind of solution will He give? Surely this verse can't be true? How can God bring any good out of this situation? With a heavy heart I went to fetch my friend from Liverpool Street Station. She was disappointed, but not too upset. "Something will work out, no doubt", was her attitude.

We had lunch in the dining room of the old people's hospital where I was living, and somehow we ended up sitting with some Christian girls whom I had never met before. We got talking with each other and my friend shared her predicament of not having accommodation for the night.

One of the girls we were talking with offered, "You can stay in my flat for those few nights. It's not far out of this area."

I couldn't believe my ears. This total stranger was offering hospitality without even being asked! Relief flooded my heart. My friend had a place to

stay overnight but, even more important, my
unbelief melted away and faith and trust grew. Now
I was able to believe even that amazing verse.

Five years after God answered that heartcry
prayer, I was living in hot, humid, noisy Bangkok,
Thailand's capital. I would stay there for a year to
study the Thai language before going on somewhere else to start the real work: church planting.

After a few months in Bangkok I had an
interview with the OMF director. He asked me,
"Are you aware of God leading you to a particular
field? Do you have a special interest in any of
them?"

For years I had been interested in the tribal work
in North Thailand and I thought I might go there,
or maybe to Central Thailand. My two-week field
trip over Christmas was spent with a Dutch
missionary who worked among the Shan people in
the very north-west corner of Thailand, close to the
Burmese border. I had a fascinating trip with lots of
"first-time-evers" such as drinking water from a
coconut ladle, bathing in the river, eating rice three
times every day, wearing a *sarong* (long wrap-round
skirt)... But although I enjoyed my time, there was
no guidance from the Lord whatsoever to direct me
to work in the north.

After a further month of language study I was on
my second field trip, this time to Lopburi, a
provincial town in Central Thailand. *Is God going to
lead me to Central Thailand?* I wondered. Once again I
enjoyed my upcountry trip and the break from
language school, but again there was no sign from

the Lord that He was leading me to work there.

I was getting impatient. "Lord, why are you silent, why don't you answer me? Why does it take so long before I know where to go?"

I had another talk with the OMF leader and I was glad that he was still willing to wait before taking a decision. I continued to pray, "Please, Lord, show me your way. Where do you want me to go?"

One night light dawned. How could I have been so blind! I hadn't been willing to go to South Thailand. I'd thought for a long time that there was only Malay Muslim work in the south, but even when I discovered that evangelism was also done among the Thai Buddhist people, it had never appealed to me to go there.

As I became aware of my unwillingness to go to the south, I realized how wrong I was. Surely Christ was my king, He could send me wherever He wanted me to go! I confessed my sin and repented of my unwillingness. Suddenly I understood why it had taken so long for God to guide me. He would rather not show me until I was willing to obey Him, for there would be no point. "Thank you, Lord," I prayed, "for showing me where I went wrong and for forgiving me."

After that things moved ahead very fast. I shared my willingness to go to the south if that was where the Lord wanted me, and within a matter of weeks my designation was arranged: South Thailand it was to be!

After I had been about a year in the south I found myself getting more and more involved in the work. I visited the Thai Christians, lent cassettes to them, went tracting with a fellow missionary and on Saturday mornings we would sell books in the market. Through the bookselling I got to know a Thai girl who seemed immediately interested in the gospel. The same Saturday that I met her she came in the afternoon to visit me at home, bringing two friends. Her nickname is "A".

"A" continued to visit me and also started to go to church regularly. After several months, I was getting a bit concerned. *Does she really understand the gospel?* I wondered. *Or does she think it's just a matter of doing the right things, like going to church?* I was concerned because she didn't have a Bible and didn't come to the mid-week Bible study, so she was not getting much spiritual food. I prayed that God would continue His work in her, and that she would get a desire to read His word.

One afternoon "A" came along and asked whether I had some time. I was a bit cautious, because the schools in town had their big annual sports event and I guessed that she wanted me to join her for the afternoon. But when I asked her "Why?" she replied, "I would like to study the Bible with you."

Wow! It sounded like music to me! Straight away she bought a New Testament and we arranged to meet the next day.

Thank you, Lord! You always answer our prayers. It might be "no", "wait" or "yes", but I believe it is most often "yes."

Kathleen Parsons, from UK, worked as a leprosy nurse in Central Thailand.

You'll get shot!

MY SMALL STATURE was greatly emphasized when I worked with Ursula and Gwen, but the presence of these tall well-built friends was definitely an advantage when we travelled in Thailand. Long legs saved a lot of falls when the motor bike slid on the muddy roads, and extra weight kept the wheels more firmly on the ground. Would-be attackers in isolated areas thought twice before approaching such westerners. But I was smaller than most nationals and I felt very vulnerable.

I prayed much about this problem, as I could not spend my missionary life in my colleagues' company. Did I trust the Lord to keep me? I realized I could, provided I was in the centre of His will. I had no right to expect His protection if I went out alone into country areas without His guidance, and so I prayed that the Lord would make his plan clear to me.

Another problem was that I was no linguist, and found Thai extremely hard. Often I used the wrong tone, thus completely changing the meaning of what I was trying to say. I argued with the Lord, "What use am I, visiting tiny groups or individuals?" The Lord reminded me of clinic patients and relatives who had become friends ready and willing to help me. They often could not walk due to ulcerated feet, nor did they have transport or the money to go visiting. But they certainly could share and encourage others, and in perfect Thai country speech. My prayer changed to "Lord, show me whom you would like me to take."

Chusee was a promising young Christian, still very shy but maturing. She was delighted when I asked her to go out with me. Her home was in a small village about four miles from Uthai town where we lived, so I would go out on my little motor bike alone to pick her up and then we would travel together to more isolated Christians or little groups in small villages.

I was amazed how well Chusee seemed to understand my faltering Thai as I shared some truth from the Bible. She would pick up the theme and share more clearly in the language the local people could really understand. We sang and prayed together, left tapes for the group to listen to until our next visit, and then travelled on to our next family or individual Christian to share with them. These Sundays were very happy and encouraging times, and it was an added joy to me to see Chusee growing and maturing in the Lord.

One Sunday when I called, Chusee was unwell but her aunt was ready and willing to go with me.

We enjoyed our trip to four villages and a few isolated homes. As we came in from the dusty rides we would be refreshed by a coconut drink or cold coffee, a bowl of noodles or a slice of fruit.

That day we had been out since 7.30 am and arrived back at Chusee's village about 4.30 pm, tired and dusty but happy. As I said my farewells and rode down the bumpy road, carefully avoiding the loose sand patches one can so easily skid on in the dry season, I sang my praises for the Lord's presence. I had travelled about a mile and just turned on to the main road, when suddenly I sensed that I was slowing down. Very soon I came to a standstill just past a few houses.

A quick check revealed the problem — I was out of petrol! Strange, I'd not yet changed down to reserve... then I remembered that a kind male colleague had cleaned out the tank for me. He had accidentally put the tubes back the wrong way round! As I looked up from the bike I saw a crowd of young people coming towards me, and soon surrounding me. It was beginning to get dark.

"What's wrong?" asked a young lad about seventeen years old.

"I'm out of petrol." The lad took the bike from me and began rechecking. Looking into the tank he said he thought there was enough to start it, and began to check the plugs. I patiently watched, conscious of the light fading.

"They're all right," he continued, as he made vain attempts to start the engine. Suddenly he turned to me and announced, "You're out of petrol", as if he had a new revelation!

"Thank you. I must get home to Uthai," I said as I took the handlebars and began to walk.

"You can't go down there!" they cried out in alarm, "you'll get shot! You need petrol. There's a pump about three miles back but it's closed today. The nearest place is Uthai."

"Then I must walk to Uthai," I said as I began pushing my bike in that direction. Again they warned me I'd get shot but, as they had no other advice to offer, they reluctantly had to let me go. I called back my thanks and assured them the Lord would take care of me.

A little further along the road I passed women working in the rice field. "Don't go down there, you'll get shot," called the women.

In my heart I was really praying as I called back, "The Lord is with me and will look after me."

The nearest woman turned to her friends with confidence and repeated what I had said, at which they nodded and prepared to go home. I set off again, praying for peace as I entered the wooded area ahead of me. I was not feeling over-confident as I faced the darkening road.

I had walked only a few yards when a light behind me lit up the way. A van stopped and the young Chinese driver asked if he could help. I weighed up this smartly-dressed man smiling down at me, and prayed quickly, "Lord, I asked You for help and I'm trusting you sent him."

"I'm out of petrol, you don't have any spare by any chance?"

The young man was climbing out of the van as the youngsters came running down the road and surrounded me again. "You've got to help her or she'll get shot!" pleaded their spokesman. In his spotless white shirt the driver reached for an empty bottle from the van. Then he attempted to undo a bolt under the van, with little success. As he tried in vain to get the petrol one young boy said, "Why don't we put the bike in the back and you can take her to Uthai?" In moments several of the group helped the man lift it on to the back. I gave the youngsters tracts to read, and they were delighted.

Climbing into the cab the young Chinese man and I were off to Uthai. We introduced ourselves and talked of the work we were doing. He owned a garage in Taptan town, and was going into Uthai on business. As we travelled I relaxed until we climbed to the top of the hills around Uthai, well known as a bandit hideout. It was now quite dark.

Suddenly lights lit up the road. It was a lorry coming from the other direction. It slowed as it neared us, and the two vehicles stopped as the cabs came level with one another. I could see four men crammed in the front. I felt rather anxious, but quickly turned my questioning to prayer and felt the Lord's assuring peace.

The men were smiling to my driver and talking of their day's work, and he in return told them who I was. As we moved off again the driver explained that the men were employed by him. He took me to the first open garage and refused the money I offered. I was also holding out a copy of St John's

Gospel, and he requested with a polite bow, "I would like the book please, if I may?" I willingly gave it and he set off to his business.

With a full tank of petrol I was soon turning into my home gate, and was greatly touched to find my two colleagues all dressed to come out to find me. We praised the Lord together for answered prayer. As I thanked them for their thought, Gwen said, "It was better to see you driving in safely."

Two weeks later one of our para-medical boys was shot in broad daylight on his way back from a medical visit, on the very same part of the road where I ran out of petrol! The bandits took his bike as he feigned death. When they were out of sight he struggled to his feet, hailed a passing van and managed to get to the mission hospital. Fortunately the bullet had missed all vital organs and he soon recovered.

Later Gwen and Ursula left and I was on my own to cover the leprosy clinics in rural areas of Uthai province. Weekends were spent visiting, and as the van was more available to me I was able to take out teams of Thai friends to encourage isolated Christians. One weekend we planned to visit several people and end up at Elephant Pool. There we would stay overnight with a very isolated lady who had been in hospital for leprosy treatment. Now she had returned home with a full leg plaster and was unable to leave her little wooden house on stilts surrounded by thick mud and trees.

All went well until we turned off the main road onto the track through the wood leading to

Elephant Pool. It was beginning to get dark and the rainy season had turned the track into a fast running river. I'd driven through rivers many times before and, remembering where the track ran, I steadily drove forward. In seconds I ground to a halt, the engine died and all four wheels sank firmly into deep red sticky mud up to the van doors!

"Try driving backward," came one helpful suggestion.

"It's getting dark," stated Jamlong.

"What can we do to help?" Pastor Yew was looking at me obviously confident that I had the answer! I could have laughed as I thought of my willing friends. None of them must get their feet wet, especially in that filthy water! Pastor had ulcerated stumps as limbs, Jamlong had recently had an operation to straighten her deformed feet, and Udom had one artificial leg.

Glancing round I saw a grassy mound protruding from the water. "Can you get out on to the dry bank?" I asked, thinking a lighter van might move more easily. As they clambered out I said, "Stand there and pray."

As they did this I took my shoes and socks off, rolled up my trousers and slithered into the slimy mud, digging at it with my hands in a vain effort to free the wheels. I was praying too. "Lord, what are you going to do to help us, please?" We were very aware of our helplessness and the danger we were in. No one stayed out after dark in that bandit-infested area. But we all had a peaceful confidence in the Lord's presence and protection.

We all heard and saw it at the same time. "What's that shadow coming from the middle of that rice field?" Pastor Yew was pointing into the dark, to where the noise of an engine could be heard. The tractor came straight to us and before we could grasp what was happening the driver was instructing me. "Start your engine, but keep your foot on the clutch and put your gear into reverse." I obeyed while he attached a convenient chain hanging from the tractor to our rear axle, jumped into the seat, winched us out back to firm land and was fast disappearing into the dark before we could even call our thanks!

My friends climbed in with amazement written all over their faces, "Where did he come from, no one has a tractor near here," said Pastor who knew the area well as he had lived in one of the villages only a few miles away. "Anyway, no one would be ploughing in this weather or as late as this."

There and then we prayed together, thanking the Lord for sending such help.

Returning along the main road we stopped at a village about five miles back and bedded down on the floor in another leprosy family's home. They were delighted to have our company and the women willingly prepared food for us with the meat I'd brought. The following morning we had our Sunday service in their tiny church shelter. This encouraged them to continue worshipping together weekly — since Pastor Yew had moved away they had been neglecting to meet. This little group was very needy, and we realized that the Lord had answered our prayer of the day before and guided us to visit those He wanted us to.

We were sorry not to get to Elephant Pool, but when we visited later that month we found it was time for the lady to return to the hospital, so we were able to take her back with us.

These experiences encouraged us all to go on praying, knowing that the Lord answers in His time and way.

Margaret Ogilvie, *from New Zealand, spent more than thirty years in Thailand.*

When God Did Not Answer My Prayer

"OUR GOD," said Dr Bryan Parry, "is a cliff-hanging God". It was the Manorom Christian Hospital weekly Thursday night prayer meeting.

Bryan went on to explain himself. "God often doesn't answer until the very last moment. You are praying for a surgeon to fill an urgent need here at Manorom. According to our way of thinking, if God sent us the surgeon now, then he could 'learn the ropes' and be ready to take over before Dr Neil Thompson leaves in August."

It was mid-May, and the hospital staff had been meeting daily since the end of April to pray about the staffing situation. Dr Wera had contacted several surgeon friends who were keen Christians. They had all replied that they could not come. What if God did not send a surgeon?

Manorom Christian Hospital was founded thirty years ago because OMF leaders felt this was God's way to introduce Christianity to an area with no other Christian witness. Five million people in the

central provinces of Thailand had never heard of
Jesus Christ. During those thirty years many had
heard and responded to the message of God's love.
Ex-patients became the nucleus of little churches in
many areas. If we had no surgeon, how could we
carry on? Could it be possible that God was closing
the hospital?

All sorts of questions clamoured in my mind as I
thought about the situation. Then I remembered a
personal experience when God didn't answer my
prayer. I was in a tight corner. Only God could
help me, but He didn't.

Two years ago a friend and faithful prayer
companion wrote to say she was visiting Southeast
Asia with a tour group from New Zealand. If she
came a week early, the last week in August, she
would have time to visit Manorom before joining
up with her group.

I was thrilled, and wrote off immediately welcoming her to Manorom. I arranged to meet her at
Bangkok airport and to spend the weekend with her
in Bangkok before bringing her to Manorom.

Early in July when information on my personal
account came through from the OMF office, I
looked at it in dismay! It was only the beginning of
the quarter but already I had spent most of my
quarter's allowance! How could that be? In OMF
our allowance is divided up into different categor-
ies. Board includes general living expenses, food,
electricity, gas, and so on, while personal remitt-
ance is for us to use for our individual needs. I
checked over my expenses over the past two or

three months. In April I had received a generous birthday gift from my sister and had "splashed" a bit, buying a suitcase, a dress and new glasses. I had had two weeks' holiday and had indulged in some extras then. There had also been other expenses for which I had not allowed.

I'll have to be really careful for the rest of the quarter, I said to myself. *Even then I don't think I can make it!* I counted out my tithing for church offerings for the rest of the quarter. Then a thought struck me. What about the thirty dollars for Christian work in New Zealand which I sent each quarter? Would it matter much if I didn't send it this time? For several days I mulled this over and over in my mind. God was faithful to me. Should I not be faithful to Him? Finally I prayed, "OK God, I'll send the money and trust you to supply my needs." So the money was posted off to New Zealand.

At the end of July I did the household accounts. To my horror I was one hundred baht short! I checked every item but could not account for the missing sum. I couldn't replace it from my personal money — I didn't have that much. Then one morning Carolyn Duncan, the medical secretary, said to me, "Margaret, I still have that hundred baht note you gave me to change. I haven't been able to change it. Do you want it back?" I almost threw my arms around her with joy. Of course! I had forgotten I'd done that with it!

As day after day went by, my supply of personal cash got smaller and smaller. I had bought a supply of stamps some months ago and still had some large denominations. So I went to Carolyn and asked, "Would you mind changing these stamps back into cash, Carolyn? I'm short of cash and don't want to draw on my account."

"Oh yes, that's no trouble," Carolyn replied.

The thought that kept nagging me was, what was I going to do about meeting my friend in Bangkok? She was depending on me to meet her. She was travelling alone and was a stranger to Bangkok. From my first steps in the Christian life I had learned to trust God for my needs. God had always answered my prayers. Why did He not answer now?

All this time, as I searched my own heart, I was not conscious of any barrier between my Lord and me. Other prayers were answered. As I worked in the hospital each day I saw Him at work in many lives. Only this prayer remained unanswered. I did not have enough money to go to Bangkok for the weekend.

Sometimes I woke in the night and the chorus based on Habakkuk 3: 19 would come to my mind. I would find myself softly singing,

> "Though the fig tree does not blossom
> Nor there be any fruit on the vine
> ... *yet* will I rejoice in the Lord
> *yet* will I rejoice in the Lord
> I will joy in the God of my salvation
> Christ the Lord is my King."

Each morning I looked hopefully when the mail arrived. Nothing. What was I going to do? Should I do as I had read of other Christians doing? Corrie ten Boom was booked to speak at a meeting in another town. She did not have the plane fare but she went out to the airport trusting the Lord to provide. There a friend met her and supplied the money she needed. Should I walk out to the bus stop and trust God to supply my need? My courage (or was it my faith?) failed. I couldn't do it.

The day before I was to travel to Bangkok, after the mail had come and brought nothing, I went to the Medical Superintendent and told him my story. He immediately advanced the money I needed. I went to Bangkok and met my friend. We had a very good time there, and then she came up to Manorom and was thrilled to see the hospital she had prayed for so long.

When the next month's account came through, an anonymous gift had been credited to my account. I was out of the red. There was sufficient for my needs until the next quarter.

I spent much time thinking over this experience. Why did God not answer my prayer? Why didn't that gift come through a week earlier? What was God trying to say to me? What lesson was He trying to teach me?

One practical lesson I have learned. At the beginning of each quarter I work out how much I have to spend each month, and endeavour to keep to it.

Several months after that experience, I listened one day to a tape by Charles Swindoll. He told this story:

"In a country area a policeman was doing his rounds on a bicycle. As he was passing a farm he noticed high up on a cliff a sheep that had fallen over the top, and was lying on a narrow ledge. He biked around to the farm house and reported it to the farmer. The farmer thanked him and said he would see about it.

"Three days later the policeman was passing that way again. To his surprise the sheep still lay on the ledge high up on the cliff face. He went along to the farmer and angrily asked him why he hadn't rescued the sheep. The farmer replied, 'I went and had a look. I couldn't put up a ladder from the bottom of the cliff as the earth was too soft. The only way to reach the sheep was from above. I would have to tie a rope around myself and get someone to lower me over. When the sheep sees two legs dangling from above it would take fright and struggle, and probably fall to its death over the ledge. I have to wait until the sheep is too weak to struggle, and then lower myself over and rescue it.'"

Was this what God was saying to me? Did He have to wait until I was ready to listen to His voice? During the previous months I had needlessly spent money without thinking, "Is this what God wants me to use my money for?" Rather my attitude had been "God doesn't deny His children anything they think they need."

I called Him Lord, but as regards money I went my own way. If He was Lord I should be asking Him what to spend my money on! If He was Lord it was His money, not mine. I should pray before spending money, not after spending it.

It is now August here at Manorom. The daily prayer meeting continues. We are still waiting on God to send the surgeon we need. But we also pray for other needs — different staff members who are ill or needy, ill patients, the evangelists in their work. This daily prayer meeting has united the Christians on the staff as nothing else has done.

The prayer for a surgeon to work at the hospital remains unanswered. Why? Can it be that God is not going to send a surgeon? Or is God — the "cliff-hanging God" as Bryan Parry called Him — going to send a surgeon at the last possible moment? When God didn't answer my prayer it was to teach me a deep spiritual lesson I would not have learned otherwise. If God does not send a surgeon to Manorom, I hope we will be able to sing with Habbakuk, "Though the fig tree shall not blossom ... yet will I rejoice in the Lord."

Lorna Edwards, *from Australia, has worked in Japan for almost 35 years.*

Much more than we can ever ask for

HOPES WERE HIGH. Inking and affixing the seals would shortly make the contract legal. Tonight the Kuroishi Church in Japan would at last own that central property on the busy thoroughfare between the post office and the railway station. It was the culmination of two years of prayer and verbal negotiation — two years of waiting for the Lord to bring to fruition what we believed He had planned for us.

But that night we experienced a strange lack of peace, and a fear of going forward. We searched our hearts and asked the Lord to open or close the door very obviously and quickly. An unexpected phone call left us with no option but to withdraw, and the door closed tightly.

We were puzzled and dazed — not stumbled or distressed but puzzled ... and prayerful. Why had it ended this way? Where should the church go from here?

We soon learned that in fact the Lord had saved

us from a very costly and dangerous mistake. And we were not long in doubt about what to do next. The Lord had kept our eyes on what seemed such a desirable property — only until His chosen place for us became available!

The very next day our fruit dealer, who also handled some real estate, appeared on the doorstep. He told us of an excellently situated travellers' inn, for which he could negotiate for us. It overlooked the same street as the place we had lost, and was even nearer to the rail and bus centres. The building itself was bigger and much more suitable than the other, but because the block on which it stood was smaller it was considerably cheaper.

We went to look inside. Because it had been a guest house the entrance was much wider than a private house one, and a spacious shoe cupboard stood against one wall — ideal for lining up Sunday School and worshippers' shoes and storing indoor slippers as is the custom in Japan. The further inside we stepped, the more surprised and thrilled we were. Several toilets, a small but adequate kitchen, the main rooms separated only by sliding partitions so they could be opened up to accommodate a good-sized congregation... there was even a tiled hotel-sized *ofuro* (Japanese bathroom with tiled tub in one corner), complete with dressing room annex and ideal for baptismal services! Fifteen or twenty could stand to view inside the *ofuro* and the rest of the congregation could witness the service from the small back garden. We went right ahead with negotiations.

Before knowing when we would be handed the key, we telephoned a Christian builder in a nearby city to come and advise about necessary work. He arrived at the very hour the land agent called us to come for the keys. We promised the builder that we would pay for the repairs in full whenever he rang to say they were complete. The morning he rang we were still ¥100,000 ($500) short. But before he arrived and while we were still praying about it, the postman came with an unexpected gift of exactly ¥100,000. The giver was a Kuroishi Christian girl just one year out of high school. Though she knew nothing about our need, she had sent her first gift of a whole year's tithe from Tokyo. We paid the builder in full when he arrived an hour later!

We were looking forward eagerly to the day when we were due to make the final payment and have the property registered in the church's name. But in a miraculous way we had the money two weeks early! Thinking that the earlier we paid, the earlier the registration would be complete, we hurried to meet the land agent and the owner and go with them to the registration office. There they discovered that, if we were to be registered tax free, we still needed a certificate from the Prefectural Office confirming that we were an authorized religious body. That status would both save hundreds of dollars now and also free us from subsequent annual taxes.

Knowing we had two weeks in hand we went to ask for that one little document, and found five other documents were needed — some from our own church, some from the mission headquarters and some from the government office in Sapporo. Even with the help of very cooperative officials, it took just two weeks to get everything together and so obtain that vital tax-free status. Right on time the document was collected, the money paid over and the property registered in the church's name.

Those first days in the new church we scraped and painted, papered walls and doors, cemented and renovated, answered the neighbours' questions, and watched the Lord supply all we needed for the day of the official opening.

Then problems began to appear. The church stood conspicuously at the head of a shallow T-junction in full view of commuters, high schoolers and all who passed by on the main road to the railway station. But that T-shaped private road also served four other houses, which meant we could not permanently park the mission car there. When we heard the house next door was being sold we prayed and asked for a narrow strip of the property for a parking space. But this time no gifts came in. Time went by and we still had only a verbal assurance from the prospective new owners that they would sell us that strip. Surely God who had seen us through thus far would not abandon us now, but why wasn't something happening?

That wasn't all. Loved members of the church, Mr and Mrs Matsuoka, had been delighted when the church had moved to the travellers' inn. It was only a minute or two from their rented house, an important consideration since Mr Matsuoka was paralyzed and couldn't be left alone for long. But now they had to move. The city had decided to support them so that Mrs Matsuoka could look after her husband without having to work and risk their both having to be sent to a city-supported hospital. But to receive that support they had to move out of the central higher-rent area to a city-provided flat where they could live on the ¥10,000 monthly rent the city would provide.

Our prayers about a parking place hadn't yet been answered, but now we concentrated prayer on the Matsuokas and their need of a house by the end of winter.

Mr Matsuoka longed for but hardly dared to pray for what seemed an impossibility — a house bigger than their present one, with rooms their married daughters could occupy when they came with their families from the south to visit. Ideally it should also have a display window facing a busy street, so that Mrs Matsuoka could display the dolls she made and sold to supplement their income. "And how wonderful if it could still be close to the church, Lord," we all added.

The snows came and almost went. Still no house for the Matsuokas and still no parking place for the mission car. Then another blow fell. The granny who lived alone and ran a children's sweets and toys shop immediately opposite the church, became depressed and took her own life right there in her house. She had been so kind in allowing us to put posters in her window, and we wondered, as we grieved, whether she might have understood enough of the message of the tracts she'd received to put her trust in the Lord.

Weeks went by. Granny's house remained tightly shut. "Will anyone be moving into that house?" we asked the neighbours.

"Oh, no! Didn't you hear what happened there? Nobody will go to live there!"

Then one day we noticed that the upstairs windows were open and the curtains flying. "Have you come to live in this house?" we asked the ladies we found inside.

"Oh, no!" replied Granny's two daughters. "We've just come to take away a few of the things that are precious to our family, and then we'll have the house pulled down. I guess you know what happened here. Nobody will live here now."

"We know somebody who'd live here if you allowed them..."

"Really? Who?"

We fetched Mrs Matsuoka to meet the ladies. "Would you really be willing to live here and look after this property for us?" they asked.

"We couldn't really ask you to let us live here," Mrs Matsuoka explained, "because our monthly rent allowance is just ¥10,000."

"Oh, we wouldn't want any rent, if you would live here and just look after the property!"

"But we would want you to take at least our rent allowance!"

To which the ladies replied, "We wouldn't ask for the money, but if you choose to pay it anyway we will cement the laundry floor and remodel the inside where the shop counters were so that your husband can use the front room and watch the busy street."

The house, right opposite the church, is much bigger than the one the Matsuokas left, and has two lovely rooms upstairs where their married daughters can be comfortable and independent each time they visit. The window that once held sweets and toys soon began to display Mrs Matsuoka's hand-made dolls, though she no longer needs to sell them to supplement her income. And behind the house was the parking space we needed — as well as a shed where we can store other things! No wonder the Lord prevented us spending a lot of money on a parking strip!

"Much more than we can ever ask for, or even think of" (Eph. 3:20) is always the Lord's measure!

Bill Merry, *from the USA, teaches at Bangkok Bible College.*

With banners carried high

PICTURE A NEGLECTED, vacant lot on a busy street in the center of Bangkok. Five women are marching around the lot, avoiding the broken remains of a long-since-demolished house. With banners carried high they are singing praises to God for what He is going to do, to the astonishment of passers-by. Two Darmstadt Mary Sisters, my wife Francoise and Margaret Pearce and Miss Achanun of the Bangkok Bible College staff, were demonstrating their faith that God would provide on that lot the much-needed building for the College. The two Mary Sisters had no hesitation about making this rather unusual demonstration of faith, but the other three in the procession had needed some persuasion, and most of the rest of us hurried off to our classes!

A building on that site seemed still a faraway dream. God had provided the money to buy this land, but we had little faith that He would provide enough to construct and furnish a large building.

The story starts several years earlier. Since its beginning in 1971 the Bangkok Bible College (BBC) had rented several houses in that area quite cheaply. However, as time passed some of them were reclaimed, rents on others were raised and it was impossible to find alternative, suitable houses. We needed a building of our own. Then a very desirable piece of land became available at an amazingly low price — about one third of the market value. The owner's mother had expressed her desire that it be used for Christian work, and her wishes were honoured.

The College Board were interested in this plot of land but no money was available. About two years passed. Now our need was even greater, and the land was still available — but at a higher price. Once again the Board considered the matter. The one important question was "What is God's will?" All agreed that this piece of land was both ideal for our purposes and desperately needed. Also, the price was still too good to be true. As they prayed and waited on God, He led them to a unanimous decision to go ahead, despite the fact that there was still no money in hand.

Within a few days a large gift was received towards the purchase price, and we saw this as God's confirmation of the decision. A contract was signed for the land allowing for payments to be made over many months. The BBC family prayed and, as each payment fell due, the money was always in hand.

The land, of course, was only the beginning.

Reaching a decision on the big question of when and how to build proved even harder. Many felt we should wait. It was a time of worldwide recession, and also other large "Christian" buildings were already underway in Bangkok. It hardly seemed right for BBC to start a project too. Then a good Christian brother reminded us of the time when the Israelites stood by the Jordan river waiting to cross. They hesitated, but as Joshua stepped by faith into the river, the waters dried up for the people to walk across triumphantly. The Board agreed that they too needed to take steps of faith, trusting God to provide at each point.

Various plans and estimates were considered. Some thought that the building should be done by stages or in separate blocks, but that was an inefficient use of the land. Finally a four-storey building was planned, filling the block of land. It would include men's and women's dormitories, a spacious chapel, dining hall, offices and a large library. The total cost of construction was estimated at five million baht (US$220,000). We did not think of borrowing money nor plan any fund-raising drive. The work would go ahead only as God provided the money.

We were at this point when the Mary Sisters visited the school on their way to Australia. A "thermometer" chart on the wall indicated the total of five million baht required. The Sisters could hardly see the red mark at the bottom showing the sum total then in hand! No matter, they praised the Lord anyway and encouraged our faith. We had started well, but now we realized it would take a lot more faith and prayer to see our new building become reality.

Whenever plans are submitted to the authorities for approval they need to pass various offices and normally, unless "tea money" is forthcoming along the way, approval may be delayed indefinitely. Again both students and faculty came to God in prayer, appealing for the plans to be approved. Our Business Manager Mr Prasarn frequently checked progress as we prayed on, and at last he was able to return with news of the final signature! Another step of faith honoured — another answer to prayer — another day of praise and rejoicing.

Enough money was now in hand to lay the foundations — no simple task in Bangkok's mushy land. Work began in late 1984 but was done incorrectly at first, which caused considerable delay while alterations were made. The foundations were completed early in 1985. Now it was time for another step of faith. Should we wait for the full amount to come in before starting to erect the building? It would be very slow and expensive to contract one floor at a time, but also impractical to start and then stop, waiting for funds. And no contractor wanted to accept a job that he couldn't plan on completing in a given time. Once again our only recourse was to pray for God to show us His plan for the way ahead. So far He had blessed and provided. Why should He not continue to do so? So we signed a contract for construction of the building, and the work began.

Payments fell due regularly as the work proceeded, and for the first few times there was no particular problem. The money was there and we paid it over. However, as the work progressed rapidly funds began to run dry. Dr Timothy Jeng, the school's director, called for special days of prayer and fasting. On several occasions time was allocated for prayer through the day, and when things looked critical prayer chains were organized. Every time a payment fell due, money was in hand! The work was never held up. Over and over again gifts came just in time, leading us into continual praise and rejoicing and providing valuable lessons of faith for students and staff alike.

As the building neared completion we needed to contract for the plumbing. This would be complex and very expensive, with the two floors of dormitories plus other facilities. Moreover, as Bangkok's water supply is not very reliable, pumping and storage facilities would be essential. With no money, but growing faith, we stepped out once more and signed a plumbing contract. Yet again God honoured the combination of prayer and faith, and the money came in when we needed it.

The time came to start electrical work and painting, two major jobs which needed to be done together. By now we had tentatively decided to dedicate the building in early March 1986, much earlier than originally planned, in order to coincide with student graduation and the fifteenth anniversary celebrations of the college. We wondered if we might now be running ahead of God!

One of the bids for the electrical work, from a new firm, was way below the others. Though naturally wanting to save money if possible, the Board wondered if that firm would be reliable, and were cautioned not to cut corners because in the long run they would certainly lose money. However, the low bidder was selected for the job and began to work alongside the painters.

By now it was close to Christmas and we began to question whether all that electrical work could possibly be completed in time. The electrical firm, eager to prove themselves competent and reliable in order to attract future customers, could not afford to cut any corners, and we too wanted a quality job. But this did mean much slower progress. Over Chinese New Year work stopped altogether for several days, leaving only three weeks for completion of the work and inspection by the electricity department authorities prior to connection. Now our prayers needed to encompass quality of work plus speed, the Inspection, and ... oh yes ... money to pay the contractor! By now, praying for the money was easiest of all!

At last the work was ready for inspection and the official arrived promptly, perhaps hoping for a nice tip. From our side he was disappointed, and as the contractor wasn't making any money on this job he probably didn't offer anything either. But the work was approved on that first visit, with the contractor being complimented on the quality workmanship.

The actual hook-up of power took more time and paper work and prayers — somewhat hurried ones, since only three days remained to the March 7 deadline, and we were up to our eyes in preparations for that. We did of course have temporary electrical service, but the water system could not function on that. On Wednesday March 5 the electrical company arrived ready for the hook-up, but they could not do it because parked cars were blocking their way! We hadn't thought to pray about that! From the early hours of the following morning determined students mounted guard over parking spaces, and the electrical company connected us up with not a day to spare.

With unlimited water now on tap, all four floors of the building could be thoroughly cleaned. I had the pleasure of throwing on the main circuit breakers and checking to see that we had power throughout the entire building. An electrician had to be called to get the large pump working, but by early afternoon on the seventh full electrical and water services were in operation. Now all could go ahead for the opening ceremony.

At dusk on Friday March 7, 1986, a large crowd gathered on the sidewalk for the opening and dedication. The white-painted building was darkened on the inside. Outside, the brightly-illuminated, three-arched facade reminded us of the triune God who had so marvellously worked in response to the faith and prayers of His people. In prayer and song we glorified God as the ribbon was cut and the building declared open. Then, as the interior lights flooded on, people crowded into the lobby and up to the large, airy chapel on the fourth floor. Seated in comfortable new chairs — a last-minute gift through OMF channels — they enjoyed the performance of a gifted harpist until the official graduation and anniversary program commenced.

We at BBC can certainly testify that God reigns and answers prayer today. And His timing is perfect. Already two of our former buildings have been reclaimed by their owners and another will soon be torn down. So we were just in time!

Moira Campbell, *from Scotland, has worked in Taiwan for twenty years.*

Setting the prisoners free

WHILE ON FURLOUGH in 1981, I wrote in my diary, "If God wants to do something more through me in Taiwan, He must teach me more about prayer first." By January 1982, He had led me to ask OMF prayer groups to pray for two things:

1) *My future work.* I had been working for twelve years with tribal (or "mountain") young folk in the church for Paiwan and Drukei people in Pingtung City, southern Taiwan. Now they needed a younger leader, and I needed another job. So I was asking people to pray that God would open up for me a full-time ministry to younger adults in Pingtung. I couldn't see how this could be done, but it never occurred to me that God didn't want me back in Pingtung.

2) The other prayer topic was for *someone to share my home,* so that it could be like a real home, and have a welcoming atmosphere.

February brought a letter from Andrew Butler, our Taiwan superintendent, asking me to consider a move to the city of Taipei, where many mountain young folk were studying or working in factories and on building sites. There were far more than in Pingtung, and they were older. But — they were in Taipei, and I had a "thing" about Taipei. I'd never really got over the trauma of my first winter of language study there in 1967, when it was so cold, grey, drab, muddy and rainy. It had rained for 42 days, with a half-hour's break one Saturday morning, during which we glimpsed the sun — and experienced an earthquake! No, Taipei didn't attract me at all!

I shared this with a prayer group I know and love. We all prayed, and they gave me feedback. Within three weeks, I knew this was God's answer to our prayers. In fact I even began to look forward to working in Taipei, so sure was I that God was going to do great things!

Late May, 1982, five weeks before my return to Taiwan, I was at an OMF conference in Scotland when a really excruciating pain struck me. Within three weeks, a cyst had been diagnosed and major surgery recommended. Five months passed before I was pronounced fit to return to Taiwan, and a delay over my visa kept me waiting long enough after that to read *The Awakening* by Marie Monsen, about revival in China. I was so inspired by it that I felt I was about to take the mountain people in Taipei by storm!

Greater Taipei has about five million people, of whom a few thousand are mountain people. About one hundred of those, in 1982, were students with some church connection, but only a handful were walking with the Lord. I'd worked with high school and college students, as a teacher and then a missionary, ever since I'd graduated from being one myself, so it seemed right to live centrally in the main university area in order to reach them.

The Lord provided a beautifully furnished apartment at less than half the usual rent for that area, within five minutes walk of two universities and ten minutes cycle ride from the mountain boys' student centre. Frank Chew of the Tsuo tribe, whom I'd met fifteen years before, had just taken over responsibility there, so it all seemed to fit together. We met each week to pray, and for me to help him with his English and share what I'd learned over my years of working with students. My part of the job was to try to locate and befriend girl students.

From various sources, my list of names grew, and I spent hours alone in my top floor apartment, waiting for those students to turn up... and not one ever did! Several frustrating hours later, I'd get a call, "I fell asleep after lunch", or "I left your address behind when I set out", or even "I'm opposite ..... University, but I can't find your lane", and they'd be miles away across the city, at the wrong university. Going out to find them didn't work out either. I'd cycle through the rain, getting covered in mud, only to find no one there. And as I went home, I would be thinking of the warm dry winters two hundred miles south in Pingtung.

I was really puzzled by this time. Before my return from furlough the Lord had given me two special promises one morning, "For the Lamb...will guide them (the mountain people) to springs of living water" (Rev. 7:17), and "Out of his heart (mine) shall flow rivers of living water" (John 7:38). That very evening a friend who was praying with me had a vision of a bed of collapsed limp plants bearing no flowers, in dry soil, and a watering can gently watering them.

"Where are those limp plants, Lord? You're giving me so much through your Word, that I'd love to share with others." My fellowship with the Lord in those days was rich, but I had a deep ache to be involved with other people.

And He said, "Oh afflicted one, storm-tossed and not comforted, behold I will set your stones in antimony...I will make...all your walls of precious stones. All your sons shall be taught by the Lord" (Isa. 54:11-13). Well, I had spiritual sons down south, but I'd been reminded to "forget what lies behind...and press on" (Phil. 3:13-14). *There must be more sons in Taipei, but where?* "I am the Lord, I have called you in righteousness...to open the eyes that are blind, to bring out the prisoners from the dungeon, from the prison those who sit in darkness. Behold, the former things have come to pass (*the harvest in Pingtung, of young people now serving the Lord*), and new things I now declare; before they spring forth I tell you of them. Sing to the Lord" (Isa. 42:6-10).

Lord, it almost seems as if you're making fun of me. Isn't this an awful waste of time? People are giving money to support me here! And back came the answer, "The

Lord will guide you continually, and satisfy your desire with good things (*honestly, Lord?*), and make your bones strong (*Haven't I been convalescing long enough?*), and you shall be like a watered garden, like a spring of water, whose waters fail not" (Isa. 58:11).

By this time I felt as if I was verging on solitary confinement. I began to pray with feeling for imprisoned Christians in communist lands. Some insight came in a circular letter from OMF headquarters in Singapore,

"God never would send you the darkness,
    if He felt you could bear the light.
But you would not cling to His guiding hand,
    if the way were always bright.
And you would not care to walk by faith,
    could you always walk by sight."

God's purpose was to teach me more about bringing prisoners out of darkness, and the only way to learn was by sitting in darkness myself, and learning how to get really involved in prayer.

Reading about the vine and the branches, I came across this: "True branches give themselves to intercession, the one great work of Christ, and the source of power for all His work." So I wrote in my diary, "What about a prayer partner, Lord?"

Three weeks later, my diary records, "Feeling it's so difficult to get into the work in Taipei, but the Lord reminded me of Isaiah 49:2, my commissioning verse when I joined OMF. 'He made my mouth like a sharp sword; in the shadow of His hand, He hid me; He made me a polished arrow, in His quiver He hid me away.'"

Lord, I complained, *what good is a polished arrow if it's hidden in your quiver? This is a very well-appointed, top-floor apartment that you're hiding me in, but "I've toiled in vain" as verse four says.*

His answer was there in verses 8-9, "In a time of favour I have answered you ... I have kept you...to establish the land...saying to the prisoners, 'Come forth'...They shall feed along the ways." That tied in with another reading that day in Luke 4, about Christ's complete victory over Satan, and how from then on He would address Satan with God's authority.

So many mountain people, coming out of animism, are in bondage to Satan, and God's preparation of me was to take time, and discipline, and learning to listen to Him. The March 15 reading in *My Utmost for His Highest* is about the discipline of dismay. I wrote, "I've been going through the discipline of dismay, and the Lord has been warning me that though I walk in darkness and have no light, I must not kindle my own fire and walk by its light. Out of the darkness will come that walking with Jesus which is an unspeakable joy." That was such a help when I went to the student centre for their English class, followed by Bible study. Exams were looming up, and they wanted neither English nor Bible. Instead of dismay, thought came, "This is significant." So home again in my top-floor "quiver", I prayed, *Lord, do you want me in student work or not?* And back came the answer, "Move to Nankang." I had been attending Jade

City Church, a congregation of the Amis tribe there, for about four months.

Then I remembered the verse about precious stones (*isn't Jade a precious stone?*) and those sons.

But why couldn't I have gone to live there earlier? The answer came through reading about Peter and Cornelius. The Lord had to use a vision to change Peter's deep-rooted ideas, before he could help Cornelius. Just when Cornelius had the need, God gave Peter the vision, and both were ready together.

Jade City's pastor had just returned from study in Korea. My diary records "God can, and will, provide a home and a fellow-worker for me." Things were moving at last. *My Utmost for His Highest* for May 8 says, "Behold, I have set before you an open door which no one is able to shut," with the comment, "A saint's life is in the hands of God, like a bow and arrow in the hands of an archer. God is aiming at something the saint cannot see, and He stretches and strains, and every now and again the saint says, 'I cannot stand any more.' God does not heed, but goes on stretching till His purpose is in sight. Then He lets fly. Trust yourself in God's hands."

So on June 1, 1982 I moved to Nankang to concentrate on Jade City, my precious stone church, where my sons would be taught of the Lord, and I was sure God would fling open the door for an exciting ministry. But nothing happened, except that the minister arranged for me to start a *young teens'* Bible class! I was already involved with the Youth Fellowship, in Bible study and discipleship training. Then a congregational meeting voted the minister out of office. No wonder he hadn't introduced me to the work of the church!

Eventually it became plain to me that the Lord wanted me there to give some encouragement to the young folk in their bewilderment at the crosscurrents of conflicting viewpoints. The "sons to be taught of the Lord" became precious. Three are now in Seminary, and another is back in his home village studying for the entrance exams. The girlfriend of one of them came to live with me, and the third bedroom was soon occupied by a sixteen-year-old orphan who had just come to know the Lord, so the prayer for housemates was delightfully answered.

Some months earlier I'd met Frances, an American non-OMF missionary with a ministry of prayer and healing of damaged emotions. The Lord had given her a burden for mountain people. When she asked whether we could pray together, my prayer partner request (as well as hers) was answered.

But I was still puzzled. Jade City church wasn't rushing to involve me in speaking or visiting. It wasn't like Pingtung! I was just "there", observing, praying for them, and doing a little personal counselling. But I began to hear of people with needs.

Jung Chin was a Tayal boy who for no apparent medical reason would have alarming heart palpitations. He had often left classes and been rushed in a taxi to a variety of hospitals, big and small. But over three or four years no cause had been found. Frances had experience and I had the language, so between us we discovered that his father had been imprisoned for embezzlement. Then, while under age, he and an uncle had "borrowed" someone's car. Uncle was killed when the car, driven by Jung Chin, went off the mountain road. False guilt from his father and real guilt from the accident did their damage within him. As we prayed for healing, he began to thrash about in real distress. Recognizing the presence of a demon, we commanded it to leave in Jesus' name (using English), and at last he opened his eyes, smiled and said, "I feel fine now."

Later he asked me, "Why did I feel as if I was being choked to death while you were praying?" Wondering whether he'd react in horror or disbelief, I gently reminded him of the boy who fell on the ground and rolled about when Jesus came down from the Mount of Transfiguration, and how Jesus had cast out a spirit. "Oh yes, that's it," he said, and smiled with satisfaction. He'd grown up with animism, so it didn't faze him at all.

May Ying is a Taroko girl who would feel exhausted, her feet as heavy as lead, every time she set off for a Christian meeting. We fixed a time to pray with her, and along she came with her aunt and her two young sons in tow. Aunt had palpitations and headaches which doctors couldn't cure, so we dealt with her first, and she was set free. Then we turned to May Ying, who had been praying quietly with us. But as soon as we started talking with her, she yawned loudly eight times, her eyes rolled up, and she "fell asleep". The battle raged for a while, and her sons added to the confusion, but they went home that night free, with praise and joy in their hearts.

Prisoners *are* being brought out of their dark dungeons, and they need to be taught, so that they can walk in the light. So now I have Bible classes to teach.

This is not the kind of work that one can do by following any set method, but only by getting instructions day by day from the Lord. Absolute obedience is necessary if we are to use effectively the authority delegated to us by Christ. But the prisoners *are* being set free and coming out of darkness. God is answering prayer. Oh yes, He *did* provide a young local leader for the teenagers in Pingtung too!

Margaret Armitage, *from UK, has worked for more than 25 years as a leprosy nurse in Central Thailand. In this story we see her also involved with her local church.*

Church camp, Thai style

Estimate:

85 seater coach	7,000 baht
Food	3,000 baht
Offering to speaker	1,000 baht
Offering to Chonburi church	1,000 baht
Other needs	1,000 baht
	13,000 baht

(about US$460)

Thirteen thousand baht, I groaned to myself as I sat in a leaders meeting in Lopburi Church.

"If this weekend is aiming at spiritual renewal, why can't we go to our local Central Thailand Conference Centre at Hang Narm and save thousands of baht?" I asked, trying not to sound impatient.

"We've been to Hang Narm innumerable times, a trip to the seaside will make it all the more appealing," answered all the Thai leaders in chorus.

One sixty-year-old man emphasized that it was

probably the only opportunity he would ever have to go to the seaside. We all laughed.

"Okay, okay!" I said, feeling suitably put in my place. I felt very rebuked that I had even thought about curtailing their pleasure — especially as I can't count how many times I have been to the beach.

After discussion on how much to charge, it was decided that 200 baht per head was a reasonable amount. As it was unlikely that the bus would be filled we couldn't just do a straight sum dividing 85 into 13,000 baht. But what about a number of our members who are very poor? We all knew they wouldn't be able to raise even 100 baht. They would feel excluded from the beginning.

Our pastor, with his usual enthusiasm, suggested that the church could subsidize the trip. Then of course the treasurer sat up with a start!

"If you wish to sacrifice your salary for a month," he suggested to the pastor, "we might manage a subsidy!" He said it with a stern face, but then he laughed.

"Point taken," the pastor grinned back at him. But he wasn't about to be squashed, and out popped another idea. "Well then, we will recommend that the richer members can sponsor someone else."

Silence. Anxious faces exchanged glances. Sitting around the table were some of the slightly better-off members, but they are by no means rich. Some hoped to go as families so I knew they wouldn't feel able to sponsor others.

At the end of our discussions it was confirmed that we would go ahead and organize a Renewal Weekend to be held in Chonburi at the end of May. We all knew it was going to be a major faith venture.

So the weeks went by. The speaker was invited, the bus was ordered, camping-style accommodation was booked at Chonburi Baptist Church. But where was the money? Lots of people said they wished to go, but comparatively few paid the booking fee.

The bus owner, a shrewd business woman, was a long-standing friend of our church treasurer. Being impressed at the radical change in his life in recent years, she trusted him. He went to see her frequently, assuring her we wanted the bus, even though he still had no money for a down payment.

We were due to leave for Chonburi on Thursday May 22. The previous Sunday we were still not sure that the bus would be more than half full. And to our dismay there was only a little more than 4000 baht in hand. Those of us in the know had very heavy hearts.

The treasurer came to see me on Monday morning looking for encouragement. He felt desperate. He was on his way to pay 2000 baht to the bus owner to confirm our booking. "Then we shall have 2000 baht left to buy food to start the weekend," he said as he sat down and put his head in his hands.

"I'm not going to Chonburi," he continued. "We are obviously going to be in debt. I shall lose face when we can't pay for the bus."

"Oh, but you must go," I said, "God is about to do a great miracle. It will be a pity to miss it if you're not there."

He looked up and grinned. He knew I was despondent too, and realized my own faith was being tested. He agreed that it certainly had to be a real miracle if we collected another nine thousand baht by Saturday night.

So we encouraged each other by remembering a few instances in the Bible where God had rescued His people from desperate situations. I told him that God had never let me down through all the years of my Christian life. Not least, we were both helped by remembering how much we had all been praying for this weekend.

As the bus left Lopburi that Thursday, there were 71 people on board, more than we had dared to hope for. Some came from other churches, and we knew they could pay the full price!

Our visiting preacher found his ministry hard going the first day, and sensed a spiritual battle raging. He told us how he felt, and gave some teaching on fasting. He knew nothing about our financial straits so this was not a gimmick to economize on the food allowance! The majority had never fasted before but, as the Holy Spirit worked, people were challenged to fast and pray during Saturday. This experience brought great blessing and real spiritual renewal, with sins being confessed and freedom in worship.

After the Friday evening offering raised less than 1000 baht, our treasurer was still gloomy. "Still no miracle," he told me. But when God deals with our hearts everything changes. By Saturday afternoon our finances were still not good, but our attitudes had changed and we were praising the Lord.

Saturday night we had another offering. There was no frantic preamble about our financial short-fall, no pressure for people to give generously. But that evening the offering bag contained over 2700 baht.

The miracle had happened. When all the bills were paid we had a surplus of 522 baht.

Sylvia Houliston *was one of the "forty-niners", the last group of missionaries to enter China in 1949. Since then she and her husband Don have worked in Indonesia, Taiwan and Hong Kong, as well as South Africa.*

Did the atheists win?

THE CHINESE GUARD glanced at our exit permits and waved us on. At the far end of the bridge men in familiar British uniforms stood waiting. Beyond them, friends had gathered to welcome us after our long journey by boat and train from inland Chongqing. We turned for a last look at the land we were leaving behind, the land to which the Lord had called us to serve Him. China was our land by adoption, but now we had to leave. The Communist liberation in 1949 had made it increasingly difficult, and finally impossible, to work with the Church there.

Saying goodbye to those who loved the Lord had been heartbreaking. How we had rejoiced over the years to see Chinese men and women come to believe and to grow in the Lord, to help train leaders and establish churches, to share in further evangelism. But the Church in China was still small numerically, not more than one million out of 800 million Chinese. Would it be able to face the onslaughts of an atheistic regime?

Our hearts were full of memories. We would think time and again in the years ahead of those friends and churches we had left. And we carried something very precious with us that day in 1951 — our prayer lists. We never stopped praying for China. Throughout the western world, missionary exiles continued their ministry in prayer. Overseas Chinese in Asia and beyond also carried this burden of intercession for their brothers and sisters on the Mainland.

The years passed. Little news came from individuals, and information about the churches was unsettling. Storms were buffeting the believers, and we continued to pray earnestly for them. Then the Cultural Revolution broke in all its senseless fury. Churches were vandalized and closed, Bibles were burned, believers imprisoned and persecuted. We agonized in prayer. "Oh Lord, how long must they suffer?"

No ray of hope pierced the darkness. The handful of refugees who struggled through brought terrible tales. Even in the 1970s after China began to open her doors again, a Christian travelling in the land wrote: "I see no trace of Christianity anywhere." It seemed that the atheists had won. Had they really achieved their objective to blot out religion? Often despairing, sometimes with little faith, people prayed on, many still mentioning individual names daily.

Politically, the worst was over. With the death of Mao in 1976 and the arrest of the Gang of Four,

China rose wearily from the shackles of the last decades and began to make friends with the rest of the world again. And, gradually the news filtered through: THE CHURCH OF GOD IS ALIVE IN CHINA! From the shadows there emerged, not a few elderly believers, but thousands upon thousands of men and women who crowded into the newly-opening churches and wrote poignant letters to the radio stations. It was soon evident that the Church had grown unbelievably.

Soon the pilgrimages to China began. Excited missionaries returned to their old haunts. "When we visited the town in which we had worked," one aged worker wrote recently, "believers came from north and south to greet us." Tears of rejoicing flowed, stories of harassment and suffering unfolded, but above all there was praise and gratitude to God who had cared for them and taught them many precious lessons. Yes, some had lost their faith, others had only recently returned to the Lord, but many more had come to faith in the midst of all the troubles.

An old pastor hurried to greet some foreign guests after a service, and asked for news of a certain missionary, mentioning his Chinese name. "I think you are talking about me," said one westerner. What excitement there was as they exchanged news of the last three decades! "You have always been in my heart," the pastor said.

"Often we consider our ministry to be *our* work. Or at least I did," wrote one pastor. "That was why I worried a great deal when I was jailed in the

1950s. I worried about my sheep: *Who is going to look after them?* I had ministered to three congregations — about three hundred people altogether. But when I was released in 1978, I found they had grown to twenty congregations, with a total of five thousand Christians!" Can you guess what that pastor was doing all those years in prison?

"During all those years they had no pastor," he continued. "But Christ Himself had looked after His sheep and caused their number to grow. Now each congregation has over a thousand people, with over twenty thousand altogether! And I can go to them only once or twice a year. Between my visits they have nobody — I mean nobody except God Himself working among them."[1]

Hudson Taylor early learned the priority of prayer in his life. The Church in China was born in prayer. So in the time of her greatest need prayer became the bulwark of the persecuted Church, hidden from the eyes of the world. Ex-missionaries prayed, the free church prayed, overseas Chinese added their pleas, and there, behind the walls of Communism, the Chinese believers themselves prayed. No westerner can equal the ardour of the praying saints of China. They met under umbrellas in the rain; while transplanting rice seedlings in the scorching heat; in the stillness of the night while others slept; they poured out their souls in labour camps and solitary prison cells.

The gospel has triumphed in China. What lies

ahead no one knows. But the Lord in His sovereign grace has chosen to use the ministry of prayer to keep faith in Him and in His Son alive in many hearts. And the mighty army that now walks the Heavenly Road in all parts of the Mainland knows that prayer is the unfailing weapon given to us by the Lord "who ever lives to make intercession for us" (Heb 7:25).

Louise Morris *and her husband Jim, from USA, have worked in Thailand for 30 years.*

Setting prayer goals

JIM AND I sat at our kitchen table nibbling New Year's cookies and discussing our strategy for reaching the Pwo Karen tribe for Christ. It was 1960, and we had been married ten exciting months. Our first home was in the Thai market town of Wangloong where we hoped to contact Pwo Karen tribal people who came into town to buy supplies, mainly salt and steel for making knives. Two young men, bilingual in Thai and Pwo, were helping us learn the Pwo language. Their names were Byt and Dyt.

We pointed to a book. "What's this?" we asked them in Thai.

"Jung," they answered.

"What's that?" this time pointing to a chair.

"Jung," they replied again.

Hey, this language is going to be fun — everything is "jung", we thought. We did not realize that they had never read a book or sat in a chair, and that "jung" meant the finger we used for pointing! They never point to an object with their finger — always with their chin!

The previous dry season had brought golden days of rice harvest and kodachrome skies. We set out to hike through the pine forest into Karen hills where village after village of Pwo people lived. The first night we had to sleep in the jungle. Byt and Dyt came along to carry our packs, and show us how to cook rice in a pot set on three stones. How refreshing to breathe this fresh pine-scented mountain air, so different from steamy Bangkok!

We reached the first village shortly after noon. The first person we saw was an old Karen man with a dirty, tattered sarong wrapped around his waist. His face was badly disfigured — we found out later that a bear had clawed it. He tottered towards us, hair standing on spiky ends, dirty, grinning horribly, holding a big field knife in one hand and a slice of dripping melon in the other. I shrank back with terror before I realized that he was giving me a big welcome. "Here, eat this melon — it will refresh you." It didn't look very appetizing with juice running down it in dirty streaks. The frogs they fixed for supper weren't appetizing, either, but we were hungry enough to eat them with peppers and rice. One lady took pity on my awkward attempts at eating rice with my fingers, and offered me their only spoon.

That night we slept on someone's porch next to a sack of rice on one side and a crowing rooster on the other — worse than a cuckoo clock. Our sleeping bags were the objects of wondering questions as the people poked at and inspected this "queer blanket"

Some villages we visited had never seen a white person before. Mothers scooped up their babies and ran screaming into their houses when we entered the village. Byt and Dyt called out "Don't be afraid". We took out the gospel records and sang "Jesus Loves Me" in their own language. Soon they peeped out to listen and gradually emerged, wondering how that little box could speak their language. "What do you feed that little man in the box?" they asked.

As we walked along the mountain ridge we looked over range after range of hills and valleys where Karen people lived. Was anyone out there in those hills interested in turning from demons to Christ?

Back in our Thai market home we regularly visited a dozen local Pwo villages, trying to break through the darkness, making friends, looking for opportunities to present Christ, the One who is stronger than the evil spirits. But no one was interested enough to make a commitment. If only we could live in a Karen village maybe some would turn to the Lord. So far they refused to allow any non-demon-worshipper to live with them — they felt it would break the tribal unity. This was the Karen way. Any deviation from Karen tradition would be considered sin.

Honk! Honk! We jumped up from our reflections to look out the door. The Superintendent's landrover was driving up to our gate. How good it was to see another missionary! Ernie and Mertie had decided to drop in for a New Year's day of prayer with us, their new workers.

We settled down with mugs of steaming coffee to share the burdens on our hearts. Ernie asked, "Have you thought of setting prayer goals for this year? We've found it's good to pray specifically. It also guides us in sorting out priorities for our work, too." After thinking and praying we decided on two goals: for the first Karen to turn to Christ, and that we would be allowed to move into a Karen village.

The months rolled around to July. One day a Karen man appeared at our door. "Can you help us?" he asked.

"What's the matter?"

"My wife just gave birth to twin boys."

"Oh, that is great! What's the problem?"

"She doesn't have enough milk to feed two babies. Can you do something?"

Maybe he wanted to give us one of the babies. We learned later that twins usually don't survive because the mother doesn't have enough milk to sustain both. Remembering the baby bottles packed in our trunk waiting for our first child to be born, I hurried upstairs to get them, then back down to the kitchen to measure out some powdered milk. Then began the lengthy explanation of how to mix powdered milk with boiled water, and how to sterilize the bottle and nipple each time. We followed the father back to his home to demonstrate how it worked. The babies took it just fine and grew like weeds.

Later, while Jim was away on a trip, a Pwo

woman came saying, "They just brought my son back from the mountains on the back of an elephant."

Well, that doesn't happen every day! I thought. "Why did he have to ride on an elephant?" I asked.

"He cut his leg with a field knife. Come see." I packed some bandages and medicines in a Karen shoulder bag and followed her back to the village. Her son, about fourteen years old, was sitting on the porch with a badly swollen leg. This was going to require more than one visit! I soaked the wound, cleaning away the pus and leaves they had put on to stop the bleeding, and bandaged it.

The next day I took along the gospel records. After dressing the leg, we listened to the songs and stories. Day after day I went back. Soon a group of children were lined up at the village entrance waiting for me to come. They began singing the songs with me. By the time the boy's leg was healed we had quite a friendly relationship and they had heard a lot about Jesus.

One day the Karen headman approached us. "We have seen how the twin babies grew and how you took care of this boy's leg. We would like you to come live in our village."

God had granted one of our prayer goals! What about the other? We had many Karen friends, but no one yet showed any signs of leaving the demon way for Christ. When we told them that Christ was stronger than the demons and would protect them from the demons' power, they argued, "That may be fine for the one who believes, but the demons would take revenge on some of his relatives who haven't yet believed. Just one person can't turn — we have to turn all at once as a group, or no one." Yet surely God had sent us to be His witness to them; surely He wanted Pwo to believe and come to know Him. We continued to pray on for the first Pwo Karen to turn to Christ.

December came — the year was nearly over. Was God going to answer? Our Superintendent wrote us a little letter of consolation: "Maybe it isn't God's time yet — don't get discouraged ..."

Then one day a man rode up to our door on his bike with an envelope. It was an invitation for Jim to preach the Christmas sermon at a Thai leprosy settlement, about five miles down the river from where we lived. We had never been there before.

When Jim arrived he found three Pwo Karen people living there among the Thai. Old Uncle Silver had been driven out of his village when they discovered he had the dreaded disease of leprosy. He and his wife had nowhere to go, until they met some Thai leprosy Christians who offered them refuge. Later some Karen accused Uncle Silver's niece of having an evil spirit in her. "You can't stay in our village — you must leave — we are afraid your evil spirit will attack us." Mrs Glass knew her uncle had found refuge in this settlement, so she fled there too, and the Thai were willing to take her in. "We are Christians. We believe Jesus is stronger than the evil spirits. We are not afraid to keep you here."

The family were very impressed with the love

and acceptance these Thai Christians showed to them. They attended Thai services and listened to Thai hymns, but they could not understand the Thai religious language. When Jim arrived that Christmas Day and began to speak to them in their own Pwo language, their faces lit up.

"You mean God understands Pwo language, too?"

He assured them that God did, and was longing for them to receive Him as their Lord. What a joy to explain God's Way of deliverance from evil spirits to people who were obviously so prepared and ready to receive this message of salvation.

Jim came home bursting with the good news. "God has answered our two prayer goals. The first Pwo Karen have turned to Christ!" What a wonderful Christmas present that was! God put those goals in our minds and brought about the answer in His time and His way.

Rhoda Inch, **from Canada, and Hanna Handojo, from Indonesia, work together in the Philippines.**

Praying against the devil's power

CUENCA IS A SMALL TOWN nestled at the foot of Mount Maculot, on the southern shore of Lake Taal in the Philippines.

We took up residence in Cuenca in early 1982, to help a small weak church in an unresponsive town. It did not seem a "strategic" place, and Cuenca Bible Fellowship was always bogged down in problems. We eventually concluded that most of these problems were linked to involvement with *albularyos* (al-boo-lar-i-o).

The term "albularyo" can be used for seers or fortune tellers, those who do massage, midwives, herbalists and spirit mediums who commune with the spirits and may do surgery without instruments. Common to all is the use of incantations and charms. People come from a distance to be treated by the more famous *albularyos*, and some are influential in local politics.

Rich and poor, educated and uneducated, young and old alike in this area visit *albularyos*. It may be first choice because considered cheaper than seeing the doctor, or just out of habit, or in desperation after all medical treatment has failed. Nearly everyone who grew up in Cuenca has gone at least a few times to an *albularyo* for treatment. People reason that their work must be of God because they use the name of God and of Jesus Christ; some write verses of the Bible on bits of paper to stick on the hurting part of the body, while others write secret words or just "hen scratch" if they are illiterate. "Supernatural power must be God's power, especially if used to heal people," they say.

Many Christians had not broken their connections with *albularyos*. Some even still allowed their children to be treated by them, or to consult a seer if something was lost or stolen.

But on the basis of Matthew 7: 21-23 we began to teach people to think again. It was not hard to see that the *albularyos* were not doing the will of God in their manner of life — most have broken homes and are just as much given to immorality, gambling and drinking as anyone else. Since Satan is also able to do miracles we must say that *albularyos'* power is from him, not from the living God. So it must be renounced along with everything else connected with idolatry, superstition or the occult.

We could feel the spiritual darkness and heaviness in Cuenca, not surprising when one considers that there are about 180 *albularyos* in this small town and its villages, plus many more in the adjacent towns and villages. But God had placed us in this situation. What was His way for us to minister here? He showed us that the key people in our church-planting ministry were the *albularyos*, and gave us a deep desire to see His victory over the occult powers.

In October 1983 we began to pray for the conversion to Christ of ten *albularyos* and to renounce the powers they used. The battle was joined, in terms of Ephesians 6: 10-18.

Within a month a new opportunity to share the gospel opened in a community five miles from our home. Some who attended our meetings told us that they had visited a famous spiritist medium who, with her disciples, had been to their area, using the same Bible as we did. We prayed against this deception and claimed the victory of Calvary to destroy the evil influence which was appearing as an "angel of light" (2 Cor. 11:14). Within a few months she stopped sending her disciples there and we heard no more about her.

A month after we began those Bible studies, the couple in whose home we met smashed and/or burned three sacks full of charms, occult books and papers, and idols. The man had been an *albularyo*.

One of those who had been interested in the famous medium was himself an *albularyo*. Already in his sixties, he became interested in listening to God's Word because of his fear of death. Nine months after he first heard the gospel from us, he yielded to Christ and destroyed the various charms in which he trusted for personal protection and power to heal people. He also renounced the incantations in his mind, and protective power (he thought) of tattoos on his arms. We learned from him that although he used paper with writing on it, this had no real value in healing people. The power was in the incantations of secret words.

This man's family had been the worst trouble-makers in the community, but that has changed a good deal, even though only his wife and one daughter have become believers.

In that same area, in early 1985, a Bible study was held regularly with several believers. Nearby lived a husband and wife plus her brother, all three of whom were *albularyos*. They began having a seance at the same time as the Bible study, and invited some who had been listening to the gospel. On February 1st, the first all-night prayer meeting in Cuenca was held, and the believers prayed earnestly about the situation. The prayer battle continued for three months or so, but finally the three quarreled and their influence collapsed. All those involved finally realized that they were serving Satan. The monthly all-night prayer meeting continues to be a blessing in the church's life.

In late November, 1985, a man living next door to the church building in Cuenca had terminal cancer. His wife called Dado, a famous spiritist, from a nearby village, to treat the sick man. He was to come with about a dozen other *albularyos*, and so a good supply of snacks was prepared for them.

One of the believers living across the street heard of this, and came to ask us to pray about it, especially as her parents still believed in the work of *albularyos*. We prayed together and renounced all the influence of these people. The result? Neither Dado nor the others ever came! Not too long afterward Dado moved away because no patients came to him any more.

In the next village to Dado's the believers had already been praying a great deal against Dado's power. They were also praying for the *albularyos* in their own village, the most powerful of whom was named Dulo. Now they rejoice that he too has lost his power and people no longer go to him. It was only in January 1986 that we learned one of the believers in that village had been an *albularyo* before his conversion seven months earlier. His specialty was to heal boils by the use of incantations. He renounced those and doesn't remember them any more.

We find it is hard work to pray for these people, renouncing all the works of the devil through them. We are grateful that God is giving us a number of believers who know how to use this spiritual weapon of prayer, so strengthening our hands. Again and again we remind ourselves and each other: with God nothing is impossible!

Larry Dinkins, *from USA, writes about some of the*
problems of his first few years in Thailand.

Didn't God hear?

AT 2.30 AM my wife and I were jarred out of a
sound sleep by the sound of someone searching
through our headboard. With a jerk we both sat up;
a thief was in our bedroom! My initial response was
to send an ejaculatory telegram to God as I
screamed out in Thai, *"Chuay Duay"* (Help, save
me). The thief, clearly flustered, waved a knife at us
and hissed at us to be quiet. But as my cries became
louder and more persistent the confused robber
decided to flee. Our imaginative guest had used a
chisel to remove half of our front door!

I can't say we hadn't been warned. A seasoned
veteran missionary had predicted that our first six
months upcountry in Central Thailand as church
planters would be the most difficult of our term.
Our friend did not claim to be a prophet, yet his
predictions were all too true. In that brief span we
would be robbed five times and spend almost a
month at hospital.

During the Normandy invasion of World War II

the allies' primary task was to establish a beach-head from which they could launch an all-out attack. The hardest fighting came during those initial assaults. Our "Normandy" was Lamnarai, a town of some 6,000 souls in Central Thailand. Early in 1981 our family had been designated to this town along with another American couple, Buzz and Ruth Curtis. As green troops with little experience, we encountered an enemy who had held sway over this town for years. Satan was not happy with our plans to establish a gospel beachhead and was not about to surrender without a fight.

Any missionary who finishes a four-year term in Thailand without sickness or some loss through theft would be considered fortunate. Petty theft seems part and parcel of life in this land. So it wasn't that the possibility of being robbed hadn't crossed our minds, but the speed and intensity of the thieves surprised us. We had been in Lamnarai just one week and had barely unpacked when the first robbery occurred. For some reason I awoke in the middle of the night and in my dazed state saw the screen door close and a shadowy figure leave the room. My initial thought was that a demon was trying to frighten us. Yet as my eyes began to focus I observed that my jeans were gone with over $200 for furniture in the pocket. In the morning I learned that the Curtis family had "entertained" the same visitor with similar results.

After this incident things went from bad to worse. Three of our team fell ill, and while we lay sick, we were robbed again! Buzz managed to get bitten by a dog and Ruth was hit by a tractor in the market. Our senior workers decided to send all "survivors" to the mission hospital four hours away, and while waiting in Emergency I overheard a doctor comment, "It's so sad what befalls our new missionaries." All in all our family spent three weeks at the hospital and a month out of commission.

On arrival back in Lamnarai we fortified our homes, hired a watchman and secured a watchdog for protection. The dog proved too fierce — it maimed two of our cats! Finally we felt secure and even wrote home assuring relatives of our safety. It was then that we heard the ominous rustling at our headboard. Both of us were visibly shaken. The slightest sound made me want to go downstairs to check our locks.

Paula fashioned a plaque with the words of Proverbs 19:23: *"The fear of the Lord leads to life, so that one may sleep satisfied, untouched by evil."*

During this time Matthew 6:19ff took on new meaning. God seemed to be saying, "Larry, hold your earthly goals with a loose hand but cling to the true treasures in heaven where rust does not destroy nor *thieves* break in and steal." Our focus on the heavenlies was intensified by the martyrdom of Koos Fietje, a fellow missionary in an adjoining province, on October 24, 1981. Koos was shot while ministering in a small village, the first such casualty in Central Thailand. Attending his funeral helped put our "momentary light afflictions" in perspective.

Days after Koos' death we were scheduled to attend a field conference and went — albeit reluctantly. When fellow workers heard of our plight they organized a special time of prayer for our two families. Seasoned missionaries who understood our fears poured out their hearts in prayer for protection and stamina. Little did they realize that at that very moment we were having our fourth break in! This time the thieves hauled off around $800-worth of goods including a cherished guitar. At this point we began to question the power of prayer. Had God not heard our pleas? Was He not concerned?

When Peter was thrown in prison in Acts 12 the situation looked, as in our case, hopeless. The turning point, however, is seen in verse 5, "...but *prayer* for him was being made *fervently* by the church to God." Halfway around the globe a small army of Christians were fervently lifting our needs to the Father. Around two hundred prayer supporters and numerous churches received our prayer letter. OMF even printed our requests in its magazine. My parents made phone calls in order to enlist further prayer support. Letters of affirmation and encouragement came from many quarters. A letter from our Home Director, Dan Bacon, was especially helpful,

"I couldn't help but think back on Paul's experience in Corinth in Acts 18, when apparently he was undergoing a great deal of harassment and stress and experiencing fear as well. In fact, from Acts 18:9, I assume that Paul for all practical

purposes had his bags packed and was ready to
leave town! Yet how wonderful of the Lord to draw
near in a vision and speak the words, 'Do not be
afraid, keep on speaking, do not be silent. For I am
with you, and no one is going to attack and harm
you, because I have many people in this city.' We
will certainly hold on and believe with you that God
does have many people there in Lamnarai who will
yet believe, and that God's purposes will not be
frustrated or aborted by thieves and robbers."

What I observed was a spontaneous outpouring
of concern and love through corporate prayer. It
was this concern and dependence on God through
prayer which had drawn Paula and me to OMF in
the first place. Monthly we had joined in an OMF
prayer group in Dallas, Texas, before coming to the
field. Now we were the recipients of the prayers of
many such groups. Surely the answer would not be
long in coming.

On December 4, a full three months after the first
break in, the police said they had a suspect whom
we would need to identify. They added, "Don't be
afraid," but that didn't keep our hearts from racing.
Unfortunately we could make no positive identifica-
tion and were sent home. A few minutes later the
police informed us of another suspect. This time
Paula paused and prayed for wisdom. The future of
a young man hung in the balance and we wanted to
be sure. God answered specifically — the suspect
was wearing one of Paula's necklaces!

During the investigation Paula had an opportunity to witness to the mother of one of the thieves. A

local Christian shared God's forgiveness and assured her that we were not angry or desiring vengeance. Later I tried to take food and tracts to the two prisoners. I was repulsed. The jailor was dumbfounded, "Why do you want to feed those animals, didn't they break into your house?" A few days later the two suspects were brought to our house to reenact the crime in our bedroom!

After a month of litigation, hours at the station and reams of reports, the two were finally sentenced. Paula and I breathed a sigh of relief. God may be slow in answering our prayers but He is never late. In just four short months I had learned more about prayer than in four years in seminary.

The main lesson we gleaned from this experience was the need of perseverence in prayer. The prophet Daniel in chapter 10 fasted and prayed for three weeks before a reply came. In our case — three months. In both cases it was importunity which was rewarded. Why is such persistence necessary? God is our heavenly Father; He saw His children in distress; why did He not act sooner? Clearly the problem lies on the human side, not the divine. The parable in Luke 18 makes it clear that God is not an unprincipled judge who must be worn down to administer justice. In our case justice was not denied, but merely delayed. Evidently we were not ready to receive the answer, and thus delay was used to train and build spiritual maturity into our lives.

Any missionary will tell you that his greatest need is a group of earnest, importunate intercessors who refuse to take no for an answer; who persevere and plead with God. Elijah pled seven times for his drought-stricken nation before the rains came. We will need to plead seventy times seven if spiritually dry nations like Thailand are to receive the cooling rains of revival.

Ellen Lister *is now retired after a lifetime of Christian service in Asia.*

Answers in red

IT WAS 1960, and I had just arrived in the town of Gopeng, Malaysia. The previous missionaries had run a flourishing young people's meeting, which I now had to take over. It didn't flourish for long. Sunday after Sunday the numbers dropped off, until there was hardly anyone left to teach. What was wrong?

I realized that I needed to wait on God, so I set a lunchtime for prayer and did not break my fast till I had finished praying for the young people. The next week the difference was tremendous! Some of the existing group came, with other new young people. And the whole atmosphere was charged with the Lord's presence.

As I continued weekly to have a special time of prayer and give God unhindered time, so numbers at the young people's meeting increased and there was great blessing.

Ever since that time, more than 25 years ago, I have continued with my weekly special time of

prayer. It usually takes the form of an extended
Quiet Time after which I have a snack breakfast. I
use a notebook, writing down the prayer requests in
blue on one side of the page, and on the opposite
page writing down the answers in red. To see the
answers being filled in in red is so exciting! My
special time of prayer always has to start with
praise and thanksgiving. It is all because of the
Name that is above every name, the Name of Jesus,
that these prayers have been answered, and something has come into being that was not there before.

After Gopeng I moved to Mambang-di-Awan.
Here there was no young people's meeting, and I
was asked to start one. Again I used my special
prayer method, and again something came into
being out of nothing. God moved the hearts of some
of the young people who lived in that difficult
village — the butcher boy, the ping-pong player,
the girl from the chicken farm, as well as the older
Sunday School children. A Christian young man
and other local missionaries helped. Week after
week on Saturday evenings young people came to
make pancakes, play games or have a musical
evening, and it always ended with a gospel message.

I was challenged by the sight of the schoolroom
in the village across the river. Every Sunday it stood
empty. I prayed, and so did local Christians and
my prayer partners back in England. And the
situation changed. On Sunday afternoons I got into
the ferry boat, armed with flannelgraph board and
pictures, and went across the river to that school-

room. Now it was no longer empty but full of up to eighty children waiting to hear stories of Jesus.

In another village I watched Chinese children lining up in the playground and filing into school. I knew there was no Christian meeting in that school. How could the gospel reach those children? I began to pray, and wrote to ask my prayer partners to pray, for permission to hold a children's mission in the school during the holidays. And permission was given! After the mission we prayed again, this time asking for permission to hold a weekly children's meeting in the school.

Time went by. One day when I was riding on my bicycle I saw the headmaster of the school coming towards me on his. We both alighted, and he greeted me. Then, holding out a key in his hand, he said, "This is for you. It is the key to one of the school rooms, which you may use for your children's meeting." So week after week the lively Chinese boys and girls of that village gathered to memorize Scripture verses, sing gospel choruses and hear the stories of Jesus.

Then there was Panny. This Chinese young lady had just become a full member of the church. One day I challenged her about serving the Lord by speaking at the children's meeting in her village. "I will help you prepare," I offered.

"It's not for me to do that," she replied. "It's your job." After this refusal Panny wouldn't speak to me for some time, even though she came most days to work in my home. I was living on my own so being "put into coventry" was very trying. I prayed, so did my prayer partners away in England. Some months passed.

One day Panny came bursting in with excitement. In her Quiet Time, she was reading Genesis for the first time and had come across the story of Abraham's servant looking for a bride for Isaac. "What a wonderful story!"

"Yes," I replied, seizing the opportunity, "and that is the very story I am due to tell the children next week. Will you tell it instead of me? I will draw you some pictures to use."

"Yes," she said, and so Panny began telling Bible stories to children.

Thank you, Lord, I prayed, *for changing Panny's mind and whole attitude in answer to my prayer and those of my praying friends!*

Later on Panny earned her living by selling simple medicines round the villages. But she would never sell anything till she had first told the people a story about Jesus.

Old Granny Shoe had accepted the Lord as her Saviour when she was 79 years old, and I visited her each week to tell her more about Jesus. Shortly after she believed I noticed the basket of incense sticks and other material used in the Chinese religion, hanging from the rafters of her thatched wooden hut. *That shouldn't still be there now she is a Christian*, I thought, but I just hadn't the power to mention it to her. Instead I prayed that it might be removed.

When I visited her again the Lord gave me power to speak about the basket, and by the visit after that the basket had disappeared.

After I retired in 1977 an American OMFer challenged me to start OMF prayer meetings and encourage prayer where there was none. Again I used the method of regularly waiting on God and expecting Him to bring something out of nothing.

The town of Keswick in England's Lake District, famous for its annual Christian convention, was brought to my notice as a place that had no OMF prayer meeting. So I prayed, and then I spent a number of rainy days visiting OMF supporters in that town. The second home I visited was a lovely bungalow. I told the lady who lived there the reason for my visit.

"Yes, I would be happy to use my bungalow for an OMF prayer meeting," she replied readily, "but I couldn't lead as I have trouble with my eyes." Then she asked, "Who are you, anyway?"

"Ellen Lister."

"Not the Ellen Lister I knew before she went to China in 1945?" she exclaimed.

Yes, I had known this lady at a young people's meeting long ago. All these years, while teaching at the Royal School for the Blind, she had been interested in OMF. Now she was retired. God had prepared her to have the prayer meeting in her home, and later she became its leader.

So many answers to prayer! And all are God's doing as He brings something into being out of nothing. "No one may boast before Him ... Let him who boasts boast in the Lord" (1 Cor 1: 29-31). Praise the Lord!

Liselotte Fehlmann, from Switzerland, has worked in Thailand for 25 years.

Letters from Home

WOULD THE OLD DC 3 be able to land on the dirt-strip airfield in the driving monsoon rain or in the smoke from the many forest fires in the hot season? We often wondered and listened for the deafening sound of the airplane that approached the airfield seemingly only a few feet above our roof top.

We were not expecting anybody and we were not planning to fly out to Chiang Mai, the main city of North Thailand. We could not afford a trip out too often, and there was as yet no road out of this isolated province near the Burma border. But three times a week we eagerly waited for another link to the outside world — letters from home!

When the plane had landed — after cows, buffalos and children had been chased off the airstrip by a specially-engaged employee — we could not wait till a postman delivered the letters to our house. We joined the queue of other impatient people at the post office to get them as soon as possible.

Fellow missionaries up in the hills sometimes had to wait weeks for their next mail delivery, and we were very fortunate to have a regular plane service. Yet we sometimes did feel imprisoned in this hilly, rather sparsely-populated province where the minority Shan people live. This feeling did not really come from geographical isolation but was something much harder to bear.

Missionaries from Australia, Scotland, USA, Switzerland and England had been working faithfully in this area for a number of years, sharing the gospel with the very devout and proud Buddhist Shan people. A few young people had believed, but most had gone back to the old ways, yielding to strong social pressure against anything new and particularly against a new religion.

Now the missionary force, never very large, had dwindled to just two single women, both only in our second term and still struggling with the Shan dialect, our second Asian language. We were mainly working with children and young people, and virtually no adults showed any interest.

Not far from our house was a shrine where the town spirit lived. Its name, written on the outside wall, is "Lord of the Iron Hand." People fear it and bring offerings. We were beginning to realize what power we were up against. How did we feel about this situation?

Judy: "I can remember feeling so defeated and wondering why the gospel didn't seem to be the 'power of God to salvation' among the Shan. I once visited a nearby village with a schoolgirl and stayed in her uncle's home. They put my bed right under the huge godshelf, and I remember lying there feeling so discouraged. None of the people we met had given me any opportunity to speak of the Lord. It seemed as if Satan was just gloating over me: 'Who are you, who do you think will ever be able to break my power over the Shan?'

"As I lay there I claimed afresh the victory of the Lord Jesus and reaffirmed my faith in His power."

Liselotte: "I had just started learning Shan after using the Thai language during my first term. But what was the use of learning to speak the local dialect? I did not know of a single adult person who showed the slightest interest in hearing the good news. I felt so frustrated. Had I been mistaken in my calling to the Shan work? Had our mission leaders made a mistake? I admit that I often compared my present work with what I had been doing prior to coming to the mission field. There I had found fulfilment and joy, and seen results. Was I throwing my life away uselessly here, forgotten in this isolated mountain area?"

No, we were not forgotten. There were the letters from home, for one thing. Looking back now we realize how much these letters, prompted by real concern and the faith of friends who had become our partners through prayer, meant to us. They assured us of their belief that in heaven many Shan people from Thailand would be praising God for

His salvation.

My mother wrote from Switzerland that she had started gathering a group of women to pray once a month in her home. This group has kept praying for the Shan for 25 years! Should such faithful prayer prove useless?

Marie, a handicapped lady in Germany, wrote letters which were almost entirely made up by quotations from Hudson Taylor. His biography was her best-loved book beside her Bible. She had been praying for Hudson Taylor's mission faithfully for many years, not knowing what had happened to it after it had to leave China. When in 1960 she met me, she was overjoyed to meet one of dear Hudson Taylor's missionary candidates. From then on she prayed twice daily for "her" missionary, and later also for the Shan people. How moving it was to visit her during home assignments and hear her pray for the Shan people just as if she knew them all personally. When she died, her very last prayer was for me and for the Shan people.

A lady in New Zealand, also now with the Lord, wrote regularly too. None of us ever met Mrs Ford, but the Lord had put a great burden for the Shan on her heart right from its beginning in the early 1950s. In her letters she urged us many times not to give up. God had given her the assurance that He would build his church among the Shan people. Her letters were always full of confident faith, even when we had to write about setbacks, about people falling back into the old ways.

Her prayer life was undoubtedly not always easy.

In her last letter to us, shortly before her death, she wrote: "Every step in God's work will be contested. As I was praying today, I was directed to a message in a book I am reading and these words hit me: 'There is no victory without a struggle, there is no perfection without perseverance.' This came from God's word to Joshua and as I read on, it was His word to you too: 'Every place that the soles of your feet shall tread shall be yours.' The feet must answer the faith. I fancy Satan does not want this to go to you, for my phone interrupts and time presses. So do please read between the lines the encouragement that I feel our Father would have you to know today."

More recent letters tell us of an eight-year-old boy in Switzerland who is praying for the Shan people, and has started to put most of his savings into his missionary bank.

These and many more letters helped us keep on trusting, expecting and working. Then, in early 1975, the whole OMF missionary team in North Thailand decided to have a special prayer thrust for the Shan work, each missionary promising to pray daily in faith for a breakthrough among the Shan people. This prayer thrust was carried on for a second year.

After that, things started happening. Fifteen people believed and ten of them were baptized. We started meeting for Sunday services in the home of one of the Christian families. Later more people believed in another area, and meetings were started there too. At long last a church was beginning.

Most of the new Christians were keen witnesses in spite of much opposition, and one young man was hoping to go to Bible school.

Then Satan attacked. Some weaker Christians turned back rather quickly when they met opposition from families and friends. Others were determined to be faithful, but then were hit by strange sicknesses. Finally, all except one couple turned back to the old way. The prospective Bible school student entered the Buddhist priesthood. They sent their Bibles and Christian literature back to us and made it clear that they did not want to see us any more. We felt utterly defeated. Was this the end of our work among the Shan?

God in His faithfulness did not let us give up. Recently our team had been doubled by the coming of a veteran missionary doctor and his wife, who previously had been working among the Shan in Burma. They were now caring for a large number of leprosy patients all over the province. as well as doing regular medical work.

One day, around this time, a middle-aged man stood at the door of the missionary doctor's house. Uncle Poo had a very alarming suspicion that he might have the dreaded disease.

"Yes," Dr Webb told him, "you do have leprosy, but don't be dismayed. There is good medicine that can cure you completely if you take it regularly."

While counting out the little white pills for the first month or two, the doctor and his wife gently told Uncle Poo that he had a much greater need than just to get rid of leprosy. He needed a Helper, a Savior to get rid of his sin and give him a new heart.

Talk about sin would in the past have left Uncle Poo quite unmoved. He had no sin, as he as a Buddhist understood sin. He needed no salvation. He was doing his best to be a good man. But now he listened. The confirmation that he had leprosy was like an earthquake bringing the walls of his self-righteousness tumbling down, for Buddhists regard leprosy as a punishment for sin in a past existence. Maybe he really did need someone to take away his sin. Who was this Jesus anyway? With his inquisitive mind he wanted to find out.

Uncle Poo was able to read both Shan and Thai, and so now he read the tracts and booklets that were given him, instead of throwing them away unread as he had done in the past. Every time the missionaries came he had a list of questions to ask, and slowly the light broke into his heart.

One particular incident gave him the assurance that this God does answer prayer. He had eaten fish for his supper, and a fishbone got stuck in his throat. It would neither move up nor down. What should he do? By this time he knew that we can call on God in any kind of need. Would God be able to help him with this painful fishbone stuck in his throat? And anyway, how does one pray to this God? How would God know that he was calling on Him and not on Buddha? He decided to place a little booklet of gospel stories on his head, and thus pray and ask God to help him. After doing this he lay down to sleep, and next morning the fishbone was gone!

Soon this family invited us to stay the weekends in their little house behind their rice fields, and start Sunday morning worship services. We could always tell whether Uncle Poo understood our teaching, because he immediately repeated everything in his own words and his own rather quaint way to whoever happened to be near. Soon he and his wife and eldest son put their trust in the Lord, and in 1979 they were baptized in a picturesque little stream near their house.

With our little faith we did not expect very much to happen after that. Uncle Poo was a leprosy patient, and many people still fear contact with them. They did not live in a village, but isolated out on their fields. But this did not deter Uncle Poo. With his big new Shan Bible under his arm, he set out to visit his friends and relatives and tell them about what he had learned. Going to the market to sell his goods, he loved to get involved in arguments about the Christian faith with other sellers or buyers. His theology may not always have been very correct, but people did hear the gospel from Shan lips, clothed in Shan idioms. Uncle Poo was very determined to remain a true Shan and pass the gospel on in a way that appealed to the Shan mind and way of thinking.

We could see that God was opening new doors in this area, so we moved in. Those early Sunday morning services in Uncle Poo's house are unforgettable. Men addicted to opium for up to thirty years, men and women with a drink problem, all sat on the not-too-clean bamboo floor in a big circle. In the centre was the inevitable pot of Shan tea drunk with a pinch of salt, and the tin of local tobacco with its strong, biting smoke, from both of which the congregation helped themselves all through the service. It was not always easy to teach through the clouds of smoke, over the din of dogs fighting under the house, babies crying, chickens cackling and being shooed away. But we did not want to make rules. We had come to bring them the good news of forgiveness and new life, not a new set of rules, of which they have plenty already.

One by one these men and women believed and were baptized. Some opium addicts were given the strength to stop from one day to the next. Numbers were still not great, but the new church included couples and families. Even though they are rather on the fringe of their society, God can and does use them to spread the gospel further.

The smoke has cleared away now! We meet in a pretty little church designed by a young man who had never seen a church building before, and put up by the Christians themselves. Here we worship God with new hymns and songs that they have written themselves.

A short time ago I talked to an old grandfather the day before his baptism. During the conversation it suddenly dawned on me that I and others in our missionary team had known this man many years ago. I remembered coming to his tiny, neatly-kept house after one of our eight-hour hikes up a valley toward the Burmese border. We were always welcome in his home, and we would gratefully sit on the bamboo floor, stretching aching legs, sipping salted tea, letting our wet clothes dry after crossing the river over sixty times — and witnessing to him.

We had to stop visiting that area and so lost contact with him. But about two years ago he moved near to one of the Christian families, who invited him to the Sunday meetings. He has come very faithfully, and listened well. The seed of the Word of God, sown into his heart, watered by many prayers, has now germinated, and he wants to be a true disciple of the Lord Jesus Christ.

The praying ladies on opposite sides of the globe have not lived to see all this. But surely they have been rejoicing with the angels over each Shan soul who has repented and been added to the church.

The battle is still on, however, perhaps even fiercer than before. The enemy is constantly attacking the little group of believers, and a number of times he almost succeeded in breaking the church up. But it is slowly growing in spiritual understanding as well as in numbers.

We don't queue up at the post office any longer. Two airplanes per day or a number of buses now bring in our mail. But we still need letters from home, letters from young and old friends who stand with us and the Shan church in the never-ending fight, and who will also rejoice with us in the victories won. What a tremendously satisfying ministry this can be! The Shan church in Thailand has been born by prayer and will keep growing through prayer.

Carol Findlay, *a nurse from USA, is now working in Korea*

An Eight-Year Prayer

"LORD, do You want me to be a missionary?"

That is a very simple prayer — but also a very important one, if you are the one praying it! I prayed that way, with variations, for eight years. And God answered, not with a bolt of lightning or a special telegram from heaven, but in common, ordinary, undramatic ways.

I had accepted Christ as Savior during junior high school days; and I had started letting Jesus be Lord during high school. Up to that point, though, I had met hardly any "real live" foreign missionaries. I went off to Bible college and began hearing more about missions. In fact, as an innocent freshman I wanted to combine the practical with the spiritual; so I chose missionary nursing as my major. I hardly knew anything about missions, but I started asking the Lord, "Do You want me to be a missionary?" That was in 1975.

At Bible college, I began to meet missionaries, and to hear their testimonies of how they had become missionaries. It was fascinating! It seemed, though, as if many had gotten a "special call" from the Lord to be a missionary. I didn't have that, so I thought I couldn't become a missionary. But I was still interested in missions; and my prayer became more specific: "Lord, do You want me to be a missionary? I haven't received any special call from You; but I am available. If You do want to use me in foreign missions, I am available." I was in the middle of college and had a five-year course to finish; so there was time for Him to guide. I waited — and continued preparing as I waited for His answer.

As I went off to nursing school in Chicago, I continued learning more about missions. I also began learning more about Overseas Missionary Fellowship. One week before college, I had started being prayer partners with a family who served in Asia with OMF; but I knew very little about the mission itself. Now, in college, I started reading their magazine and occasionally attending some of their prayer meetings. I continued to say to the Lord, "I am available for missions service," even though I still hadn't received this "special call" that many missionaries talked about.

When I broached the subject of being personally involved in missions with my parents in Michigan, at first I got a somewhat negative response. "Why can't you stay and be a misisonary here in Tuscola County? There are plenty of opportunities for service right here," my father said. My parents are believers; nonetheless, their response was understandable. I let the matter rest, knowing that there was time enough for things to change. I had to finish college and could wait. If *God* wanted me as a missionary, He could change my parents' attitude.

After nursing school, I returned to Indiana for a final year of Bible college. At that time, the opportunity arose to go to Sierra Leone, West Africa, for a few months working at a mission hospital. After prayer and getting my parents' approval, the signal was "green" for "go;" I left in June of 1980. The question was still there: "Lord, do You want me to be a missionary?" And my simple word was still there: "Lord, I am available." Actually, the question had changed a bit over my college years; now I was asking, "Lord, can I be a missionary for You?!" I had learned much about the need for missionaries; I had heard of and read about some of the challenges and joys of missionary life. Now my attitude had changed; I wanted to be a missionary. And the Lord knew about this; He had probably brought about the change.

So I went off to Africa for six months. Before, during and after my time in Africa, I was still saying to the Lord, "I am available for missionary service." And before, during and after my time in Africa, it seemed as if the Lord was saying to me, "Go ahead and apply to a mission board. You've been telling Me that you are available; now tell that to a mission board." When I returned from Africa, my parents were more open to the idea of me going as a long-term missionary. I think the Lord used the short-term experience to show them that I was *seriously* interested in missions. The six-month period in Africa had also been a "trial run" for us. Could they handle having their daughter so far away for so long? Could I handle it? We both passed the test.

I returned to the States in December of 1980. During the first weeks of 1981, I wrote OMF about application. They replied asking me to talk first with my home churches, to see if they supported my going with this interdenominational, evangelical mission. One of the churches replied within a short time, pledging their support, but the other took two or three months to reply. I continued to pray. "Lord, may Your will be done in this situation."

At this time, I was living and working at a hospital in Fort Wayne, Indiana, where I had gone to Bible college. And now a friendship with a young man from the Bible college began to develop. He was headed toward service for the Lord, but at home, not overseas. The friendship grew... so by the time I did receive the word of approval and support from the other church, I was not free within myself to proceed with application, and it was "put on hold".

Now the problem wasn't external but internal. So, that summer and fall, my prayer had yet another variation: "Lord, should I pursue application or not? What about this relationship?" I was still very interested in missions; and I still believed that I would be involved in foreign missions... but I didn't know how all the details were going to work out.

Week after week passed. Finally, about six months after I had gotten the word from the church, the friendship changed — from being "special friends" to "just friends". That was Christmas of 1981. One day early in 1982, I was down praying again: "Lord, what do You want me to do about the mission application?" Then it struck me: I was free to move ahead!

So, I started (almost "again" it seemed) with the application process. As I worked on all the papers, I prayed: "Lord, if *You* want me to be a missionary with this group, then may I be accepted. And if You *don't* want it, please *close* the door and let me not be accepted." I believed that God could and would guide through the decision of the mission leaders.

Around the end of 1982, I finished filling out all the application papers. I was doing further nursing studies, so I didn't have to hurry. Early in 1983, the mission invited me to their next candidate school. This in itself was a promising sign, because they invited only a limited number of applicants. I went to candidate school that summer ... and was accepted by the US Home Council as a missionary with Overseas Missionary Fellowship!

That was an exciting time. Up until the day of acceptance, I did not know if *God* wanted me to be a missionary. The prayer of a college freshman eight years earlier had simply been, "Lord, do You want me to be a missionary?" During college, it had been modified: "Lord, do You want me to be a missionary? I don't know right now, but I am available." Then it had changed a bit again: "Lord, *can* I be a missionary for You?!" Along the way, different things came up that could have seemed like "problems", from the human point of view: parents' initial opinion about missions; slow response of a home church; a friendship with a young man not headed towards foreign missions. BUT GOD ... But God was faithful during the whole time. God answered my prayer — in His own time and in His own way. I believe He answered and guided through the decisions of the mission leaders at candidate school. God guides; and God does answer prayer.

Barbara Irwin, *from New Zealand, has worked in Central Thailand for over ten years.*

Prayer power displayed

IT WAS EIGHT AM on Monday morning. Our day off. Gwen Kay was just settling down to write letters and I was pottering in my room. Hearing a visitor chatting to our Thai housemate, Laiat, I popped downstairs to say hello. It was Wat, one of the Christian young men.

"Barbara, can you come and see Mrs S?" he asked urgently. "She is possessed by an evil spirit and needs our help."

After prayer, Gwen, Wat, and I took the short walk through the rabbit warren of back lanes to Mrs S's primitive little wooden house. We met a distressing sight. Mrs S was sitting on a rough bamboo slat bed rocking back and forth crying "Torment, torment ... I want to go to Bangkok ... torment, torment."

We tried to speak to her. "Barbara and Gwen have come to see you."

"I don't know them."

"Jesus Christ can help you."

"I don't know Jesus. Torment, torment, torment. I want to go to Bangkok ... torment oh... oooh... torment." The rocking back and forth continued.

Teenage daughter Kim had a rebellious look about her. "Mother has been like this since yesterday," she told us unwillingly. "It is a spirit which possesses her for eight or nine days each year." Kim had a spirit string around her neck to protect her, and she waved it at her mother. "Mother is afraid of this spirit string." Mrs S recoiled in obvious fear.

"Kim, Jesus has power," we said gently. "He can set your mother free from this evil spirit. Do you want us to ask Jesus to set her free?"

"No, I don't." We three Christians looked at each other. We felt helpless in face of the strong powers of darkness. What do you do when someone doesn't want to be set free?

After praying briefly we returned home. Wat went back to his nearby house, and Gwen and I went on talking about Mrs S.

"It doesn't seem as though we can do anything." said Gwen, sounding depressed. "They're not wanting to be set free so we're powerless."

"But are we really powerless?" I queried. "I don't think we should just let this pass. What about all of God's promises. And after all Mrs S did show some faith in the Lord earlier this year, even though she seemed to turn back to Buddhism afterwards."

So we looked at God's Word, to see what Jesus did. In the story of Jesus healing the Gerasene demoniac in Luke 8: 26-39, we noticed the demons asked Jesus not to send them into the abyss, but begged to be able to enter the pigs. It seemed Jesus not only ordered the demons out of the man, but also told them where to go.

"We then must tell this spirit to go to hell where it belongs," we discovered.

Then we thought about Jesus' words in Matthew 18:18, "Whatever you bind on earth shall be bound in heaven, and whatever you loose on earth shall be loosed in heaven." We had the right to bind this spirit and expect it to be bound.

"And there's the fantastic promise of Matthew 18:19," I remembered, "'If two of you agree on earth about anything they ask, it will be done for them by my Father in heaven.' And another promise to claim is Mark 16:17 'And these signs will accompany those who believe: in my name they will cast out demons.' That's plain enough."

"Let's remember the basis of authority on which we act," Gwen cautioned. "We go and confront this situation not on our authority, but Christ's. In Matthew 28:18,19 Jesus said, 'All authority in heaven and on earth has been given to me. Go therefore...'"

"Yes, we go because of His authority," I agreed. "Let's claim these promises and ask God to give us the faith to believe Him in this situation. Without faith we'll be like the disciples in Matthew 17: 14-19 who couldn't cast out the demon ... But then Jesus said to them in verse 20, 'For truly, I say to you, if you have faith as a grain of mustard seed, you will say to this mountain, "Move from here to there," and it will move; and nothing will be impossible to you.'"

"Let's pray."

So Gwen and I spent time in prayer. We praised God for His promises, and asked His help to be able to stand upon them. We also asked Him to increase our faith. We then covered the situation in prayer, asking God to bind the powers of evil in Mrs S's house and to take the rebellious attitude from daughter Kim so that she might want her mother to be freed. We confessed our own sinfulness and asked for the protection of the blood of Christ.

"I'll ask Wat to come back and join us at noon," said Gwen. "It would be good to have him with us, and Laiat too."

Midday saw Gwen, Laiat, Wat and myself seated at our dining table. We were just about to pray when Green, another Christian lass, arrived. So she joined in too.

When we reached Mrs S's house things seemed to have changed. The powers of darkness were somewhat subdued, and Mrs S was now lying peacefully on the slat bamboo bed. Kim was sitting with her. But she kept interrupting our attempts to converse with her mother, so finally we asked her to sit on the other side of the room with a group of her teenage friends. Mr S was also there.

So with the non-Christians (including a few spectators) on one side of the room and the five of us Christians gathered around Mrs S on the other, we began to pray.

Unitedly we thanked Jesus for His power. Then

in the name of Jesus Christ of Nazareth we ordered the spirit to leave Mrs S and go to its rightful place in hell.

Mrs S began to shake violently. She called out, "Go, go, go." A few moments passed and she lay back peacefully, opened her eyes and greeted us as though we'd just arrived. She was obviously physically weak and exhausted.

We then challenged Kim. "That spirit string you have. It's of no use to you and needs to be burnt. Please let us burn it."

"No, I'll burn it myself later. It's OK, I really will." But the devious look in her eye made us doubt.

"In the name of Jesus Christ of Nazareth give me that string right now."

She handed it over and we burnt the thing.

We suggested to Kim that she get something for her mother to eat and drink, and let her have some rest. She hadn't eaten for a day, nor slept the previous night. Gwen read some reassuring verses from John 10 about no one being able to snatch us from the Father's hands. Then after further prayer for her protection we left.

How we rejoiced as we returned home at this demonstration and experience of God's power. My faith had taken a ten-foot leap forward that day. At the same time we remembered Jesus' words to the seventy, "Do not rejoice that the spirits submit to you, but rejoice that your names are written in heaven" (Luke 10:20).

Gwen was particularly impressed by the unity

which had bound the five of us together as we prayed. "Surely it is prayer of people in agreement that God honours!" she had learned.

The next day Laiat and I went to visit Mrs S. What a transformation! A bright smile was on her face as she greeted us, and the look of torment and darkness had completely gone. We questioned her, and found she couldn't remember anything about the previous day.

Did she really belong to the Lord or not? If not, she was in a very dangerous position indeed. We had to find out.

"Yes, I believe God is the sovereign Creator of all. Yes, I've heard about Jesus on the radio and from you. Yes, it is good teaching."

"But have you confessed your sins to Christ? Have you invited Him into your life?" Despite our sharing the gospel some months earlier it seemed she had not yet taken this step. So Laiat and I carefully explained the way of salvation and challenged Mrs S with the need to be born again. Her husband gave us his full attention too, while Kim lounged on a hammock and listened with half an ear.

On our return home we prayed hard that Mrs S would accept Christ, and for the protection of their house from all evil forces.

Two days later Gwen and I visited again. We found Mrs S physically weak, probably from exhaustion and lack of food, but spiritually alive. Yes, she had accepted Christ! What a joy it was to hear her whisper a prayer to her new-found

Saviour. Mrs S was eager to listen again to the gospel. Kim's manner had changed too. Gone was the rebellious attitude. "I've taken down the white string from around the house now. I realized it was useless in protecting us from evil spirits," she said. I noticed she was no longer wearing the customary Buddhist charm around her neck either.

In heaven the angels were rejoicing over the salvation and deliverance of Mrs S. But God's work in this family was only just beginning.

In her physical weakness Mrs S wanted her grown children to come and visit her. So a day or two later I had the joy of meeting up with her married daughter Mrs Somsak. Gwen and I had been praying for this young woman for the past four months, since at her last visit she had shown the beginnings of faith. We had heard her husband was opposed to Christianity. However, when he heard how Jesus had delivered his mother-in-law from the evil spirit, his opposition turned to interest.

The couple willingly accepted my invitation to come to our house and see gospel filmstrips. We were able to present the gospel to them, and chat in friendly fashion as we waited for the heavy rain to stop. They told me how to get to their home in Bangkok.

About two weeks later Bangkok missionary Christine Buckley and I travelled to their home. They welcomed us warmly, and we were thrilled to see that the idol shelf was empty.

"I haven't worshipped idols or made merit for the last four months," Mrs Somsak told us. "I pray to Jesus every day, and I know He is real. Did you bring the Scripture and teaching tapes you promised?"

"Yes," I assured her, "and a tape of Christian songs too."

"Will you be able to come to our church on Sunday?" Christine asked.

"I have to work on Sunday," Mrs Somsak said, "but my husband is free."

Christine gave Mr Somsak instructions of how to get to the church, and made arrangements to visit Mrs Somsak to teach her regularly.

As I continue to pray for this family, I realize they have a long way to go from these first faltering steps to become mature members of Christ's church. The promise I claim for them is Philippians 1:6, "He who began a good work in you will carry it on to completion in the day of Jesus Christ."

Many people saw Jesus perform mighty miracles, but did not allow His power to transform their lives. This seems to be true with Mr S and Kim. Mr S is a slave to alcohol, and Mrs S has now moved to Bangkok for a time to stay with a son and escape her husband's drunken ranting and raving. For Kim, at home with her father, the quest for fun and pleasure with her teenage friends dominates her life. As we pray, may they find in Jesus the living water which satisfies forever.

Ann Flory, *from the USA, began the Mangyan Christian Elementary Schools in the Philippines.*

*No more
purple
people*

"MY ... NAH-YIM ... iss ... Dyon," he said, hiding an embarrassed grin behind his hand. Uan (John) was trying out the English sentence he had learned in the "fun class" at the training session for volunteer tribal teachers. Aside from being able to count in English, this was all he knew, for English was not a part of the curriculum for the teachers of the Mangyan Christian Elementary Schools, Mindoro, Philippines.

My introduction to Uan was a note I received about the prospective teachers: "Uan Yagusnai, 21, married to Bagunia, and infant. More constant than the other Tawbuid teacher-to-be. Will teach combined Fandung-Dalandan School." I first saw Uan when he arrived with the group of g-string-clad men and mini-saronged women at the first teacher-training session.

When I noticed that Uan held his books sideways, I knew what his position had been around the one-per-family primer in the reading class taught by his missionary! Like the other three prospective teachers he had never been inside a school building and knew nothing about teaching children. But that would soon change.

"Color the trees green, the flowers red, the sun orange, the sky blue and the people brown." Sounds simple enough for any four-year-old, right? Wrong! In the culture of these tribal teachers-to-be only four colors were recognized: red, black, white and blue-green. So at the beginning of our training session, trees might be colored blue, the sky green, the sun red and the people purple!

Learning how to teach the difference between "da" and "ga" in the primers and how to write these syllables was easier for these prospective teachers than learning how to teach the skills of jumping rope or playing dodgeball. Adding two bamboo sticks to two more would also be easy for them to teach. But teaching or even singing the Filipino school songs which were part of the curriculum was a different matter! Even at the end of their training, tunes were unrecognizable.

Two months later, I visited each of the four new schools. As I watched Uan, standing before his class clad in a g-string, a once-white T-shirt and a safety-pin earring, I realized he looked much less like a teacher than the young man in the neighboring tribe who wore well-fitting trousers, an ironed shirt, and even had his hair neatly cut and combed.

"Who is making a noise back there?" teacher Uan asked his 29 pupils. "You be quiet and listen. How many of you still don't know these syllables?

Raise your hands. You will be the ones to read them now."

I was fascinated. *This isn't my training*, I thought. *Uan is just a born teacher.*

After teaching for a year and a half, Uan approached me. "My family and I are planning to move to Safa Village," he said. "Would it be all right for someone else to teach here in my place?"

I was stunned. "Is there someone else?" I asked, thinking, *I'm losing my best teacher.*

"The Dalandan and Fandung churches are praying about that," he replied in an effort to cheer me up.

Later the churches decided that each village should have its own school, and chose two new teachers who would need to be trained. But what about Uan? He could train them!

During his last term of teaching there, the newly-appointed teacher-trainees sat in on Uan's class every day. After a few weeks they took turns teaching, first one subject, then two, until each was able to teach a whole day on his own. Later, when I visited one of the two new schools, I smiled to myself when I heard, "Who is making a noise back there. You be quiet and listen." Uan had done a good job!

By the time Uan moved to Safa Village, where there already was a school, the number of pupils in that growing village had jumped from 22 to nearly twice that number. About half of these students still could not read, so the class was divided. Uan taught the slower students and soon they were brought up to the reading level of the others.

Long before my furlough I realized that these budding schools would still need supervisory help while I was gone. At one of the training sessions I asked Uan if he would be willing to take my place during my furlough. The perplexed look on his face said, *Do you think I could do what you are doing?* I quickly explained that I would finish the materials, so his job would be to keep the schools going and to give the teachers their thrice-yearly training.

"Besides," I said, "we still have a year and a half to work together so you can learn. I feel the Lord has led me to choose you." He then agreed, and that night during prayer time he asked his fellow teachers to pray for him.

Earlier than expected Uan had his first experience of training teachers without my help, for emergency surgery kept me out of the hills. He came to me to review the lessons and pick up the materials needed before going to the three schools to instruct the teachers. Gunye, one of the teachers he had trained, went along with him as a companion. By the time I went on furlough, a year later, Uan was an experienced teacher-trainer.

When I remained in the States after my furlough, Uan wrote to me, "The schools are doing fine, but five other villages now want schools. There are not enough materials. We are praying that you will come back." And I did.

Uan continued to train the teachers while I plunged into the task of revising materials and making more copies of each chart, flashcard and teachers' manual. Gladly I relinquished my travelling in the hills to Uan, for he was as capable as I at training and much better at trekking. He was even able to discover the reason that one school had stopped functioning. The teacher told him that he was fed up and did not want to teach — which he would not have admitted to me.

Uan had been faithfully training teachers for several years when one day I received an unexpected note from him.

"I can't go to Occidental Mindoro.

I can't even walk now because my foot is very swollen. Uan"

As I wrote to my prayer-partners I thought, *Now what will happen? How long will it be before he can walk? Could I even find the trail to the village where he is to teach, let alone make the strenuous trek there? I can't do the training and still prepare all the materials!*

But God answered prayer for Uan and gave me new guidance. When Uan was able to travel again, I suggested that Gunye should begin helping with some of the training. Uan, always a few steps ahead of me, said with his sly grin, "I thought about doing that before but I didn't know if you would approve."

This arrangement worked so well that soon Gunye became the leader of a team of his own, training another young man to help in the teaching. Uan also took on another trainee. But still Uan was the only one who could take care of problems that arose, set up the schedule for teacher-trainers, and begin new schools.

When it was time to begin training the teacher in one of the schools, the team would arrive at my doorstep on the appointed day to pick up the materials I had ready for them. So I was surprised that Uan and his partner failed to show up at my house at the designated time for their teaching trip to Dyangdang. After several days and still no Uan, I hiked up to his home in Safa to discover the reason.

What a shock! I didn't recognize the thin young man with sunken cheeks sitting in the doorway. Only by the grin on the yellow-hued face beneath the shaven head was I able to recognize the Uan that I knew. He told me he was still not back on his feet after three weeks of chills and fever, and that his head was shaved to get rid of lice. I knew he would need a long period of recovery. Dejectedly I returned home to send an SOS to my prayer partners.

Sending Gunye in Uan's place to train the Dyangdang teacher was not as difficult as sending him to start the new school in Sinariri. It was always Uan who started new schools. This time I would need to depend on Gunye. I hoped that he had learned enough by working with Uan to be able to do this taxing job, for he lacked Uan's confidence. But I needn't have worried. When Gunye and his partner returned, they eagerly reported that the new teacher understood all they had taught him (and they didn't think they had forgotten anything). He would begin classes the following week.

With joyful relief I was soon able to write home,

"Uan has completely recovered and has even made the arduous trip to train teachers on the far Western side of Mindoro."

As I continued to revise materials, making charts and flashcards and mimeographing new teachers' manuals, the teachers were being trained by a team of instructors which had now expanded to six. Confident that everything was running well, I was not worried when my work took me away from my home for a few weeks. Returning, I was jolted by the news that Uan, suffering from a bleeding ulcer, had been carried from his hill home to the nearest hospital. "I knew I was dying," he told me later. "The bleeding just wouldn't stop."

Friends at home, though unaware of his condition at the time, had been praying for his health. And God again restored him.

By the time I had the materials ready for the Western Tawbuid schools, not only was Uan able to go there to give further training to these teachers but he was also busy, while at home, with his banana business and his tiny store. And he was learning to accept and make allowances for the times of illness he would probably continue to experience.

About three hundred tribal children who otherwise might not even be able to read have now received a four-year education through the work of Uan and his team of teacher-trainers. Because these schools have not received government recognition and only exist where there are no other schools, the children are not able to go on to higher education.

But many of them have gone on to the tribal Bible School. And even the ones who have not, have become more effective members and leaders of their churches and communities. It is the prayers of God's people that have made all this possible.

Recently in Uan's own village of Safa I held a series of seminars for the teacher-trainers. During the first one Uan was so ill that he could not attend a single class. However on the last day, with his wife's help, he prepared a thanksgiving feast for those who had studied. Doubled up with pain and leaning on a walking stick, he hobbled to the school house to lead a simple service before the meal was served.

The Safa church had heard about the celebration the night before. Uan, too weak to stand up in the church, had written a letter for Gunye to read to the congregation:

"Our dear elders,

This is my word to you. We don't want to hide from you the fact that we will have a little thanksgiving tomorrow. It is all right if you come and watch this conclusion of our studies.

1. We are very thankful to God because we have not been able to count all His goodness to us during these sixteen years.

2. We are thankful to our white friends, too. Though we have never met some of them, they have helped us.

3. We are thankful to all of you for your cooperation during these sixteen years since June 1970 and for your children who have studied.

4. We are thankful for you young men who have taught and the many others who have helped.

5. The thing we are most thankful for is answered prayer.

Now continue in your praying which results in blessings that are never ending.

Thank you,

Uan"

For the full story of the planting of the Tawbuid Church, read **BEYOND THE GREAT DARKNESS** by Ann Flory's sister, Barbara Reed.

Barbara Wibberly *and her husband Gerald, from USA, have worked in North Thailand for over twenty years.*

A unique year

UNUSUAL PROBLEMS and disadvantages threatened to swamp the 1985-86 school year at Phayao Bible Training Center (BTC) in North Thailand. Less than three months before the school year was to start the staffing needs were acute. Our regular director, Mr Somsak, was still doing further studies in England, and his substitute was about to go on furlough. In addition to this, the dorm mother of several years had suddenly resigned, owing to the critical illness of her step-father in South Thailand.

The BTC administrative board had an emergency meeting in March 1985 and, lacking any alternative, appointed OMF missionary Gerald Wibberly, my husband, as interim director for the coming year. He'd been on the staff for six years as a teacher, and had sometimes acted as dorm father or dean of studies, but he didn't feel that administration and leadership was "his cup of tea." We asked our prayer partners to pray he would have special wisdom for the year ahead.

Jerry's first job was to find some more staff before June. What about Mr Arun, a university graduate who'd spent two years at BTC and had planned to study theology in Singapore, with a view to some day coming back to teach at Phayao? Obstacles to further study had come up, he had married his fiancee, and was now looking for a teaching job in the Northeast where his wife had a good job as a nurse's aide. Would she be willing to leave it, we wondered, and would he be willing to come and teach? Within a month we had an affirmative answer.

Good dorm mothers are hard to find. Someone highly recommended a young lady named Jampa. She had experience working in a Bible school in Northeast Thailand, and had just finished a year of studies at Bangkok Bible College. We tried unsuccessfully for about a month to locate her. Meanwhile our prayer partners were bringing this need to the Lord.

In May we finally located Jampa in Bangkok. She was not thrilled at the invitation to Phayao, since she already had good prospects of a job with a church in Bangkok, and anyway wanted to get away from working in a school. However, it was odd that every time she tried to contact the person responsible for the job possibility, she was either on vacation, sick in the hospital, or "out". The more she failed, the more Jampa had to consider whether the Lord was leading her to BTC. She fought against the idea, but some OMF missionary friends in Bangkok urged her to be open to God's will, even if it went against her feelings.

Finally, still failing to reach her Bangkok contact, Jampa made God a promise. If she phoned Phayao, in response to Jerry's repeated invitation, and he was available to speak to her, then she would accept the position. He was, and she did, with the assurance that it was God's will.

So our prayers for a dorm mother were answered, and more than answered, because Jampa was an experienced teacher as well. We didn't know just how invaluable she would prove to be until, later in the year, two of our seven teachers felt led to leave BTC and go into church work. Jampa was indispensible in helping to fill the gap, as all of us also had to take on heavier teaching loads. Her skills also included leading a choral group, which we had no one else to do that year. Her counseling gift, her charismatic background and her balanced and tolerant attitudes were a great help in the problems we faced later in the year.

A few weeks before school started, the staff met for a few days of fellowship and planning. We were challenged anew from Colossians 1:28 that our aim was to present every student "perfect in Christ." We prayed that the opening meetings and all the events of the school year would work out most effectively to do that.

As usual we had invited a special speaker to preach at two or three days of inspirational meetings at the beginning of the school year. However, just a few days before the students arrived, we received a telegram saying the speaker had had a slight accident and couldn't come! We would have to do the best we could ourselves, with three of our male staff members sharing the preaching. Feeling the need of a special night of prayer for this, the staff and some of the students who'd arrived early met on Friday night for praise and intercession together. The next day most of our seventy students arrived, and the opening meetings began.

During the Sunday morning meeting, led by Mr Sayan, the Lord began to work. Mr Sayan sensed the Holy Spirit leading him to invite all who had problems in their lives to come forward and ask God's help. About twenty of these young adults responded, and were taken to other parts of the campus to be counseled in pairs. Apart from those who found assurance of salvation, a variety of other problems were dealt with.

The two girls I was randomly assigned to counsel both experienced definite answers to prayer as a result of this session. One was worried because she didn't have funds to pay for this, her second year of Bible school. The other girl, a Chinese shopkeeper's daughter, had extra funds, and immediately volunteered to contribute the sum needed. This Chinese-Thai girl, on the other hand, was distressed because her non-Christian parents had strongly opposed her coming to Bible school. In our time together she received comfort and assurance that she was in God's will, along with advice to write a conciliatory letter to her parents. Within her first few months at school their attitudes became much more positive, and later in the year her mother came to the Lord.

Another result of these opening meetings was the new spirit of enthusiasm for worship and prayer which continued for most of the school year.

During the summer vacation and in the staff retreat we had been discussing the need for a vital church to be started in Phayao town. A church building already existed, situated in the compound of a European mission which had its headquarters and children's school there. But there were few members, no church workers, and no outreach or growth. It served mainly as a place of worship for the BTC students on Sunday mornings.

At the end of May, Mr Sayan attended a conference at which he became fired up with a vision of starting a new church. In June he began taking steps to make this a reality — renting a building, recruiting helpers, and leading several people to the Lord. Later in June, a pastor from Bangkok came up and conducted evangelistic meetings in an unused movie theater, with the result that dozens of young people and a few older ones made professions of faith or showed interest.

In a wonderful answer to years of prayer, our house girl, Bee, was one of those who made a commitment at those meetings. She had worked for us and other staff for over fifteen years, but had never shown more than polite tolerance when the Lord was mentioned. For the last two years we had been especially praying for her salvation. In her village no one showed any interest in Christianity, so she had to be willing to go against the current. Subsequent changes in her life and attitudes, her faithful attendance at church, and her hunger to know God's Word have proven the reality of her conversion.

Many of those who made professions of faith later met up with opposition and drifted away, but about thirty members now remain, almost a year and a half later. It has not been easy. Visions of scores coming to Christ in a short time have given way to the reality of patient, sacrificial labor with few results. Still, in a town many had written off as "gospel-hardened," with only one or two conversions in ten years, this was truly a notable answer to prayer.

Unfortunately, this blessing carried with it some negative effects. Some extreme charismatic doctrines were being stressed. Many students as well as some of our staff were being strongly influenced by them. Some found a closer relationship to the Lord, but we felt that many were just hopping on the bandwagon, seeking a spiritual or emotional thrill. A distinct gap appeared between "pro" and "anti". Some were urging their "experience" on everybody and feeling persecuted if moderation was suggested, while others were made to feel like second-class Christians. Each side was critical of the other.

We didn't believe the Lord was pleased with this lack of love and unity, both within the school and between the school and the church. Also, as an interdenominational, OMF-related Bible school, we have always kept a moderate position.

During this time of conflict Jerry found himself in the middle, trying to make peace and to keep things balanced. Constantly the situation was committed to the Lord in prayer.

At this very crucial time John Davis, founder and former director of BTC, was making a brief visit from England. His testimony and teaching to the students was perhaps more effective than anything else would have been in toning down excesses and straightening out thinking on extreme doctrines.

Not long after this, the leader of the new church came to the BTC administration to confess wrong attitudes and ask forgiveness. This was a big step forward in rebuilding tolerance, love and goodwill. This spirit increased as the second half of the school year progressed, and continues to this day. The solution of this critical problem reflected the prayers of many, both in Thailand and in home countries.

Near Christmas of that school year another prayer was answered in an unexpected way. Mr Arun, our new, hardworking teacher, had been praying for his non-Christian brother-in-law, Khempet. Shortly before Christmas, Khempet was released from military service and came to visit his sister for a few days before going home to look for a job. The spirit of love and peace at BTC got to him, as did the witness of students and staff. He decided to prolong his stay and to go out with Arun and the band/drama team, who were to spend a week or so evangelizing in Northwestern Thailand during the Christmas break.

Many were praying for Khempet and, much to everyone's joy, he gave his heart to the Lord during the early days of the evangelistic trip. Immediately he joined with the team in giving testimony to his faith. After the break, he still couldn't pull himself away from Phayao. He asked the students to pray for God's leading in his life. He felt a tug towards Christian service, but his parents wanted him to get a lucrative job. Before the end of the school year in March, he had become convinced that he should enter BTC as a student and prepare himself to serve the Lord. His gifts in leadership and music have already contributed much to the school as I write in November 1986.

This unique school year came to a climax with our annual conference and graduation in March 1986. It was timed for earlier than usual, before the public schools started their summer vacation. In previous years many young people had come; would the early date mean a much lower attendance? A few days before the conference, one of our teachers had a dream that nobody showed up on opening day. This led him to call for a special time of prayer. When the big day arrived, several hundred people registered, most of them adults.

Every detail of conference went well, including the musical numbers led by Miss Jampa, the excellent speaker, and the graduation ceremony.

For the staff, it had been a year of proving the Lord's grace as we received strength to carry an extra-heavy teaching load, to cope with the loss of two fellow-workers, and an often confused atmosphere during the first half of the year. Jerry certainly received wisdom for the director's duties beyond his experience and natural ability. Problems were resolved, souls saved, and God's kingdom progressed. In all these things many people had a chance to cooperate, through prayer, with the Mighty Mover of the universe, Lord of the Church.

Mertis Heimbach *and her husband Ernest went to China as missionaries in 1946. They later worked in Thailand, and now have a ministry to Asians in the USA.*

Lord, if you want me to keep this baby ...

"LORD, if you want me to keep this baby, please take away these pains," I cried. I thought I couldn't take any more. I was four months pregnant with our first baby, and Ernie was doing his best to help me keep up with our soldier escort. We had been forced to travel from the Black Miao tribal village back to our former mission station in the Chinese city of Tuyin. This was China 1950, and since the Communist takeover the year before the country-side was not yet fully subdued, although the cities and towns were under control. Moreover, it was just before Chinese New Year when brigands were particularly active. We had begged local officials to let us stay a few more weeks before returning, but they replied, "No, you have to go *now*!"

So we did go, and we were robbed. But a Communist officer took pity on us and gave us an escort! The thirty men had started off at quite a pace, fearful of attack by the brigands who were anxious to increase their dwindling stores of ammunition. We had just come through some of the most dangerous territory, when the leader of our little troop called for a fifteen-minute rest stop. God was wonderfully answering my prayer! I was able to stretch out on the ground and fully relax.

As I lay on the ground my mind went back to a verse of a hymn —

"How good is the God we adore,
Our faithful, unchangeable Friend."

Was it only the night before last that God had strengthened us through these same words? It seemed much longer. So much had happened since. We had been waiting for a truck to take us to Tuyin, but when one came the driver refused to take us. If we stayed in that little village another night the robbers would surely hear we were there. My faith was gone. I had reached rock bottom and felt God had forsaken us. I couldn't pray with Ernie. Then the phrase of that hymn came to me.

"We'll praise Him for all that is past,
And trust Him for all that's to come."

Well, I thought, *in future days we will look back on this experience and praise Him. So I might as well praise Him now before it happens, and trust Him for all that's to come.* Then Ernie and I prayed for a good night's sleep, and we slept in peace.

It must have been around 4 am when we were awakened by the landlady of the inn where we were staying.

"Get up! Get up! The robbers are coming!" she called, as she banged on the door. We had been told not to go outside without the landlady. We got up quickly, but there was no landlady anywhere to be seen. Soon a man came in and asked,

"Any tobacco?"

"Look in the back room," we suggested.

The next thing we knew he was outside shouting, "Foreigners here! Come quick!"

The room filled with men. The leader, a gun in each hand, pointed them at us.

"Take off your clothes!" he ordered.

I took off my padded Chinese gown, and Ernie his fleece-lined jacket. Just then they found our baggage and their attention was turned away from us. What amazed us was that our hearts were perfectly at peace, without fear. Ernie took courage to ask for our passport which was in his shoulder bag, and I asked for my gown back. These things the leader gruffly returned to us.

"The fifteen minutes are up. Time to go!" the Communist leader called. My reverie was broken and I was back in the present. I got up from the ground. My pains were all gone!

After that the soldiers didn't go so fast. They soon stopped in a village to buy rice for the noon meal, which they would have to prepare for themselves. We had no money, so asked permission to go on ahead at our own pace. Nearly twenty miles further on we reached the mission station at Tuyin — rest and safety! Doris and Cyril Weller, fellow CIM missionaries, welcomed us with open arms. After a day in bed I felt like a new person, and a suitcase of clothes from the Wellers replenished the clothing we had lost to the robbers.

I knew that in a few month's time I would have to go to Guiyang, the provincial capital of Guizhou, for the birth of my baby. By local bus the trip would take at least a day, but no buses were running. Arrangements would have to be made. Meanwhile, the fellowship was delightful. But the days went by all too fast.

"Ernie," Cyril called one day after getting home from church visitation, "I heard the Post Office truck got held up by brigands. Some passengers were shot and the mail burned. It's too dangerous to travel without a military convoy."

It was then decided that Ernie and I should try to get to the capital as soon as possible. Since travel was so uncertain, we had better not wait till the baby was nearly due. Doris, a nurse, gave me a book on how to prepare for an emergency delivery, cautioning, "It won't hurt to be prepared."

I read it carefully, and followed its suggestion to make up a little kit of sterilized gauze and equipment. We were prepared now to leave at a moment's notice, as soon as we got word that a convoy might be leaving.

"Get down to the Post Office truck by 4 am tomorrow," a Chinese friend informed us one day. "We hear the convoy could be leaving." We were there well before dawn, sitting on the Post Office truck waiting for the military convoy to start moving.

Several hours later the sun had risen, but it didn't look as if anything would happen. Ernie was called away to counsel a believer having marital problems, leaving me alone on the truck. While he was gone the Post Office truck began to move! I protested strongly.

"He'll catch up," they replied. "We want to leave ahead of the convoy. Our truck may break down, and this will give us time to repair it before the end of the convoy passes us. It's dangerous to be a straggler at the end."

So there I was, pregnant, alone, with no money and no passport, in an unescorted truck heading out toward bandit country. Sure enough, we did have to stop for some tinkering. Just then a man from the Post Office came up on a bike.

"They're not going after all. You'd better come back!"

The next morning we tried again. This time the convoy did leave and Ernie was with me. He was locked in the back with the mail bags, while I was on the front seat between the driver and his assistant. The trip was bumpy and I was feeling none too well; even so I was glad to be on our way at last.

Every once in a while the driver would look back to see if the convoy was in sight. After some time I noticed he was getting worried.

"I can't see the convoy! How stupid of me to get so far ahead," he moaned.

The rough ride in the truck had brought on light contractions, but according to the book I realized it was "false labor", something many women experience several weeks before a baby is ready to arrive. Sometimes there were several in a row at irregular intervals; sometimes they would fade away completely. It was still six weeks before my due date, so I didn't worry.

The driver need not have worried either, for it wasn't long before the convoy caught us up again. Toward evening we stopped at the small town of Guiting, and soldiers dashed out in every direction. Ernie rushed to find a place upstairs in a small inn where we could lay our bedding mat on a board platform. The door wouldn't shut completely, but at least it was a place to sleep, and we were thankful.

That night, about midnight, the pains returned, in earnest this time. We had heard there was a Chinese Christian doctor in town who had fled from a Lutheran hospital in North China. The Communist move west finally caught up with him and he had set up a clinic in Guiting. Ernie set out to call him, but the soldiers on guard would not let him pass.

"There's a strict curfew on," they said.

"But my wife's having a baby and I need to get a doctor."

"That doesn't matter. No one is allowed on the streets for any reason!"

Ernie's heart started to pound as he came back upstairs. As he cried out to the Lord, peace came, and he calmly set about making things ready. Stepping over sleeping soldiers in the hallway outside our door he went to see if he could get some boiled water.

"No, we have no boiled water, but we have warm

water. The fire's gone out for the night."

"What about a wash basin?"

"No, we can't let you use any." (Anything connected with birth is considered unclean to the Chinese.) "But you can have a wooden foot-washing tub." It was a fairly new tub and we figured it had not been used for too many dirty feet.

The only light we had was a small oil lamp similar to those used in Bible times. It had a shallow cup with a pith wick at one side dipping into the oil. Seeing our light, a soldier came into the midst of proceedings wanting to light his pine torch from our lamp.

Soon a wee little boy, Daniel Roy, made his appearance. We dressed him up in a little shirt given us by the Tuyin evangelist's wife, and wrapped him in a little quilt she had also made. As first light dawned, Ernie called our doctor friend and we were taken to his clinic. What a contrast to our poor little inn. Here were real beds made up with brand new crisp sheets — surplus given them by the US Navy when they were in Peking.

But little Daniel Roy was premature and only weighed 4 lbs 10 oz. And due to our lack of experience, the cord had not been tied tight enough and he had lost blood in the night. His small face looked like a little old man. My own hand was large enough to cover the length of his back. He turned blue three times the next day, due to loss of blood and inability to keep his own heat. So we put him in bed between me and a hot water bottle. He was fed with mother's milk every few hours, but this had to be done with an eye dropper since he had not developed sucking powers.

What a comfort it was for me to read God's Word that first day while the life of my baby hung on a thread. Isaiah 44:3 became God's word to my heart, and put my heart at peace.

"I will pour out My Spirit on your offspring,
And My blessing on your descendants."

Later, in the evening of that same day, I could hear two men on the sidewalk outside my window. They were talking about an "unlucky" baby. Had it not been for God's promise to me, their words would have put fear into my heart. But I had been shielded by God's Word. They did not know my baby had the special blessing of God upon him! God wanted me to keep this baby. He had special plans for him.

Now Daniel Roy, with his wife Anna, is serving the Lord in Washington D.C. Jonathan, his first child, was born in December 1985. On his hand-made wooden cradle Daniel has written this same verse from Isaiah 44. God's blessing is being passed on to our descendants.

Waltraud Hornig, from Germany, has worked in Taiwan for 18 years.

A door that opens

A DAY OFF. I need to get out of this polluted place once in a while. A bus takes me up a tree-lined road to a hilltop. How clean and orderly everything is up here, so spacious, green and quiet. Can it be true that only a twenty-minute bus ride separates me from that other world?

I walk over to the ridge to get a glimpse of Hsin Chuang — New City — stretching out below me. Life must have been pleasant on that fertile plain between the silvery flow of Great Han River to the East and the lush green mountain range along its western border. Now a quarter of a million people are depending on that same space of land for their daily food. Thousands of grey four-storey flats are pressed together between 1,700 factories on only nineteen sq km. Eighty thousand workers keep the wheels and conveyor belts running, feeding container after container with products labelled: Made in Taiwan.

Somewhere down there, in the middle of the

hustle and bustle of modern industrial life, more than ten churches are trying to gather together the Christians who have moved into Hsin Chuang from other parts of Taiwan. Most of the churches are very young and small. I'm still waiting to see their outstretched arms reaching into the neglected industrial communities to offer the bread of life. I wish I knew more Christians on the management level and on the shop floor who could be catalysts between the churches and the factory workers. But everybody is so busy — the company demanding overtime work to meet deadlines, the workers appreciating overtime work or even another evening job to help pay off their flats and all the odds and ends that go inside.

Somewhere down there too is one second-floor apartment serving as a gospel center. For more than a year now Jeannie Kang, a staff worker of the Taiwan Industrial Evangelical Fellowship (TIEF), and I have tried to contact the churches and encourage them to care for factory workers. We also try to reach the factory workers directly: in the center by teaching skills and through the library and recreational and evangelistic programs; outside the factory gates with a monthly TIEF publication called *The Friend of the Factory Worker*. We have seen about ten young people from the factories receiving Christ as their Savior. But what about all the others who don't come to the center? Will they get a chance to hear the gospel? We should get inside the factories. But how? There are too many restrictions.

Somewhere down there towards the Great Han

River, which has lost its silvery glow and is carrying ugly muddy dead waste water, there is the Lien Chang Electronic Company. I remember it very clearly ...

I leaned my bicycle against the Lien Chang gatehouse for the first time about nine months ago. Grabbing my bag with a good supply of the *Friend of the Factory Worker*, I introduced myself at the gate: "I come from the gospel center. We have a good monthly publication, free of charge, which helps the factory workers to settle easier at a new place and gives some practical answers to their problems. I would like to distribute it outside your factory. Here is a copy for you to read." The gatekeeper received it politely and I continued, "How many workers do you have? When do they finish work?"

"We have about three hundred people here," came the reply. "They get off at 4.50, in just a few minutes' time."

I waited outside the gate. As soon as the bell went, doors opened on three different floors at once and young boys and girls in their white uniform jackets rushed down the outside staircase. As they went through the daily routine of punching their cards their minds were running faster than their feet, choosing a supper dish at the cheap street restaurant next door.

Of course they hadn't expected a foreigner with an outstretched hand offering free literature, but they took it anyway. The three hundred leaflets were soon gone, and so were the workers. Nobody stayed to chat, and I had no chance to say more about the gospel center. It was the same yesterday at the San Yang Company and the day before at the World Electronic Company. Is it worth it?

I needed God's special travelling mercies as I cycled back to the center through the heavy traffic, praying: "Lord Jesus, please cover each piece of literature with your blessing. Let them read it right through and see the advertisement for the film next week at the center. You need to free them from working overtime, you need to move them to come along."

Jeannie and I passed out 2,500 copies of the *Friend of the Factory Worker* that month at over ten different factories. We got only one reply.

The month passed quickly. I was back outside the Lien Chang Company with a new issue of the magazine. The bell went, the white jackets appeared. *Will somebody stop to talk?* My hands passed out the leaflets as the young people pressed through the gate. I tried to establish eye contact with some, smiled, sometimes even managed a verbal invitation to the gospel center.

An elderly gentleman outside the office building seemed to be watching me. After a time he walked over and asked for two copies. Then before I knew what had happened he was gone. *Most likely their security guard*, I thought, *watching out for improper literature getting inside their factory*. I had met them at almost every other factory. "Please Lord, let him be in favour of this publication. Continue to bless this company, their management, their workers. And if there are Christians inside, please let them get in touch with us."

During the following month we prepared for the new three-month term of classes to start in March. We used our best artwork and had the invitations printed, ready to be passed out with the next issue of the *Friend of the Factory Worker*. I asked my prayer partners to pray for this new term.

Once again I was outside the Lien Chang Company. On the dot of 4.50 the place livened up with the young single factory workers. They looked bright and intelligent, full of life ... This company produces high quality electronic equipment and requires skilful and conscientious workers. Most of them are senior high school graduates, who didn't make it into university.

They rushed through the gate, grabbing my leaflet. *But what's happening — can it be true?* Some of them actually stretched out their hands, wanting a copy! That doesn't happen too often. Then that gentleman came again asking, "Can I have two copies, please?" *Of course he can have two copies, but what is he doing with them?* Before I could pull myself together to start a conversation with him, he was gone again.

Jeannie and I met as usual at the self-service Chinese restaurant behind the gospel center, to get a quick supper on a plastic plate before the evening's activities started.

"Jeannie, I sensed more friendliness at the Lien Chang Company today," I told her. "Some actually thanked me for the leaflet. And the gentleman was there again. Let's concentrate prayer on that factory. I hope to get a chance to talk to that gentleman next time. And now I think of it, not a single copy was thrown away! You know how many we had to pick up yesterday outside the World Electronic Company!"

First day of the new term brought new faces, new names, and new hope on both side. The student: *Will I be able to remember some of my school English and dare to talk?* The teacher: *Will I be able to make it interesting enough for them to enjoy each lesson, stick to it and hear the gospel during this term?*

I took a special interest in three girls from the Lien Chang Company. Their new English names were Ina, Jeannette and June. They liked to stay behind, were interested in the library and even offered to help pass out our leaflet next month.

When that day came I prayed several times during the day: "Please Lord, let me meet that gentleman again, and give me the right words to approach him." Ina saw me first. "I'll take some copies inside, she offered. "Some are staying on for overtime work." She disappeared behind a door, where I am not allowed to go.

Where is that gentleman today? I wondered. I couldn't see him anywhere. Soon the place was quiet again. As I cycled home I should have been praising the Lord for Ina, who had become a vital part in my ministry, carrying the Good News where I couldn't go. But I was disappointed that I hadn't had a chance to speak to that gentleman. *Lord, why haven't you answered my prayer?*

It was the same situation a month later. Jeannette and Ina both offered their help in passing out the leaflets. There were more friendly faces, more smiles, more hands stretched out eager to get a copy. But no sign of the elderly gentleman. *Why was he so eager to get two copies each time before, and why don't I get any reaction from him?*

We had a good time at the May First Labour Camp. My three friends from the Lien Chang Company had brought two more colleagues along. Together with 160 other factory workers they were exposed to the gospel in a lovely green fresh-air environment. Jeannette, usually the shy one in the English class, made a comment that set chords of praises ringing in my heart. "Our boss must be like you," she said. "When he addresses us on a formal occasion he often adds, 'We have lots of reasons to thank our God for His goodness.'"

"What is the name of your boss?" I asked her.

"Chang Gen Fa." In my mind I saw that elderly gentleman. That must be the boss! Mr Chang Gen Fa — a Christian? That was more than I dared to hope for. If he was, what kind of a Christian would he be? I had met some with a very weak testimony, who thought only of their own advantage.

After May 1st, Mr Chang Gen Fa's name was put on my daily prayer list. I informed my prayer partners abroad about the Lien Chang Company, and at our monthly OMF prayer meeting in Taipei I asked people to concentrate prayer with faith on this factory owner. And many people started to pray with us. Recently a letter from a prayer group in East Germany asked what was happening in the

Lien Chang Company, and assured me that they were praying for Mr Chang Gen Fa. During the following weeks I felt more and more led to pray for Mr Chang's spiritual life, that he would experience the riches of Christ.

Each month, when I prepared to pass out the leaflets again at the Lien Chang Company, I went with expectation and prayer that I would meet Mr Chang. I wondered if I should ask for him, or give him a telephone call. But God did not lead me to do that.

July brought a change in the staffing of the gospel center. Jeannie Kang was replaced by Shirley Pan, also working with TIEF. In addition, Janie Chen joined us as a social worker. She was full of ideas and enthusiasm. As we went over our annual plan together I explained the situation at the Lien Chang Company. "I believe God has already chosen that factory and will open the door for us to go inside by September," I told them. "We need to continue to pray for Mr Chang and for a way to get in touch with him." And suddenly I could see it: I wasn't to approach Mr Chang informally outside the gate, but rather we should make a formal visit at his office together.

It wasn't easy to get an appointment. But God gave us another chance to meet Mr Chang informally. A daughter church of a big Baptist church in Taipei City was opened opposite the Lien Chang factory, and we learned at the dedication service that Mr Chang had contributed substantially towards the purchase of the building. The pastor of this new church offered to introduce us to him. We exchanged name cards, and he told us to get in touch with him later.

More inquiries from abroad arrived: "What is happening in the Lien Chang factory? We are praying."

The day came when busy Mr Chang could fit us in. Daniel Tsai, Executive Secretary of the TIEF, accompanied us at this first formal visit and explained the structure and aim of TIEF, especially the function of the gospel center. Mr Chang had interrupted an important business meeting. He looked so tense, so old, so tired. I prayed quietly in my heart: "Lord, he needs your joy and strength. Let this meeting be refreshing to him. Let him have the courage to put your kingdom first."

After about twenty minutes Mr Chang was on our wavelength. Twenty minutes later still, he was getting excited about our suggestions we had made and coming up with some ideas of his own. "I'm not the kind of person to preach the gospel", he said, "but I'll support you in every way, as long as the working process is not being interrupted." We could assure him of that, since all our activities are planned for the off-work time.

Mr Chang opened wide the door into his factory. "Use the dining room for your activities. You have freedom to visit in the girls' dormitory. You can set up a library and get tapes to play during working time. You can join us on our annual outing and arrange a program. And of course, I will be responsible for all expenses."

Then he had to rush back to his unfinished business meeting. That was important in human eyes, but with our continued prayer the result of our first meeting with Mr Chang will have everlasting fruit.

Thousands of shapeless, crowded, grey houses, dormitories, factories in Hsin Chuang on that stretch of land below me. A quarter of a million people, 80,000 of them inside the noisy, busy factories. What chance do they have to hear the gospel of hope, of abundant life in Christ?

"Thank you Lord for people concerned for them. Thank you, Lord, for adding Mr Chang Gen Fa to that team. Thank you, Lord, for doors opening into the factories. Please give us more open doors."

Terry Pye, *from UK, is Superintendent for the OMF team in Korea.*

Understanding Jonah

BEFORE WE EVER WENT to Korea we heard a lot about missionaries who couldn't wait to get back to the field at the end of furlough. Thoughts of them filled me with gloom. A brighter memory was of another OMFer who once said that he wished it was four years at home and only one year on the field! Now that was more like it! (Needless to say he is no longer on the field!)

We had enjoyed furlough so much and the Lord had given us so many opportunities to serve Him. It had been a marvellous year. But now it was drawing to a close. A letter had already come from the OMF office in Sevenoaks telling us that our return tickets were booked, and if we were unable to use them there would be considerable financial loss. Deep inside me was nothing but turmoil. I knew that the Lord's call to Korea had in no way been revoked, but to me it had the feel of a prison term that was not yet served and I did not know how many years it had yet to run. All I could think of was how wonderful it would be to be allowed to stay in England. I understood Jonah more than ever before, as I shared his desire to get on a ship going in the opposite direction.

Time after time, I laid out all my objections before the Lord. My greatest battle then (and now) was the Korean language. After one four-year term my command of it was still poor. In February 1977 on Orientation Course in Singapore, when I met one of the directors for the first time, he exclaimed, "What! Aged 35 and from Lancashire and going to Korea! I don't envy you!" Actually I didn't envy myself either! I had gone to Korea knowing that it was going to be an uphill struggle, as I had enough battle with English. However, I had clung to the promise that "He who calls you is faithful and He will do it" (1 Thess 5:24), and I interpreted this to mean that He was going to give me the ability to speak Korean. Instead, I had experienced four years of tremendous frustration, seeing others progress while I felt as if I was trying to climb a mountain with sheer slippery slopes. Few people seemed to comprehend how disheartened I was. Could I really face another four years of it?

Then there was my mother. She had found the parting the first time so traumatic and had become very ill soon after we left. Could I really do it to her again? I knew how much she loved her grandchildren, and how seeing them go would break her heart.

So the prayer that I longed for the Lord to answer was, "Don't make me go back to Korea,

Lord. Please let me stay." Turmoil, longings, prayers and struggles were a daily inward reality. Not really the sort of thing you share as you carry on with a deputation programme! Few people would have realized how I was feeling.

Then one November morning, a letter came from our Superintendent Peter Pattisson in Korea, hotly pursued by another letter from Alan Mitchell (then Area Director for Japan and Korea). As I read them, a sort of sick feeling welled up inside. "Would you be prepared to go back to Korea and take over the superintendency of the field from Peter?" they asked.

"Oh no, Lord!" my cry went up. Here I was longing not to have to go back at all! All my objections came flooding in, now twice as strongly. To become Superintendent after only one term on the field was crazy. To do it with inadequate Korean was impossible ...*and what about my mum? ... And I'm not like Peter. I don't have his kind of experience. I'm not that kind of leader...* There were no end of reasons why the letter was "ridiculous"!

That morning the post had come early and I had not yet spent my time with the Lord. After reading the letters, I wasn't at all sure I wanted to get up and face the day, yet I wasn't much in the mood for an extra hour in bed. "Lord, what am I to do?"

My Bible reading for that morning was Exodus 4. As I read it, I saw myself in Moses, arguing with the Lord. "What if they do not believe me or listen to me?" Here was Moses arguing his lack of experience and leadership qualities. Verse 10 came straight from my heart. "O Lord, I have never been eloquent, neither in the past nor since you have spoken to your servant. I am slow of speech and tongue". "But Lord, this lack of language is getting me down. If I go through another four years of battling with this lot it will finish me off! Why me?!"

How did the Lord answer? "Moses, I'm going to work through you. You are going to do great things with my help ... They will listen to you ... Moses, didn't I make you, even your mouth?"

"O Lord, *please* send someone else to do it" (verse 13). Boy, was Moses reluctant! — so was I! Then the Lord was very angry with Moses. Was the Lord angry with me and all my objections too?

I read on through the chapter. With some trepidation, it seemed to me, Moses told Jethro about wanting to return to Egypt. Even then he did not tell him the whole truth (verses 18-20). But Jethro's reaction was: "Go, and I wish you well." I think it must have been a great relief to Moses when Jethro said, "Go in peace." The Lord had prepared the way for Moses. He had prepared his father-in-law's attitude.

As I read on that morning, it was as if the Lord was saying, "Terry, I've heard your prayers over these past weeks. Here is my answer ... NO! You cannot stay in England. You must go back to Korea. I have work for you to do there. As I was with Moses, so I will be with you." I noticed too in verses 21-23, that it was only as Moses stepped out in faith and obedience with the Lord that the Lord shared His plans with him, and they had sweet communion together on the journey.

And so it came to pass that in January 1982 I returned to Korea. As in 1977 it was an act of faith and obedience, and once more I was undergirded with a promise from the Lord. I am writing this four years later, on the brink of another furlough. How has the Lord kept me in these years?

When we return to England my mother will not be there. She was wonderful when we left in 1982, and a lot braver than the first time. But in December 1983 she became very ill and asked to see me. I returned to England to spend three precious weeks at her hospital bedside. Not until the night before I had to fly back to Korea did I learn that she was dying of leukemia.

During those three weeks we talked about the Lord. One day she said to me, "I always wanted a faith like yours and your Dad's, and now I have it. When your Dad died (1967) I came to rely on you. But then you went away so I've had to find the Lord for myself, and I have." I had wanted to stay in England partly for my mum's sake, but the Lord sent me back to Korea and made mum His own child. Two months later she went to be with Him. The Lord had prepared her heart.

During my Quiet Time that morning in November 1981, the Lord surely answered every one of my objections as I put them before Him. To me the Korean language is still an unattainable mountain top. The slopes remain unclimbable ... in fact they seem a lot more slippery. At times this gets me down. Yet the Lord sent Aaron to be Moses' spokesman and Moses had at times to rely on Aaron to do the talking. I cannot tell how many times I have to rely on others to help out. I wonder if Moses found it as frustrating, humbling and humiliating as I do? Yet it was God's way for Moses and I can only conclude that it is God's way for me. I am so grateful to all the Aarons who help me out, even though I still fervently wish I didn't need them!

I can't tell any stories of the staff in my hand turning to a snake in order to persuade the team that I am God's appointed leader, but maybe that's because I have not needed to! They have at all times been wonderfully supportive and understandingly tolerant of my shortcomings and limitations.

Furlough! Yes, what a blissful thought... to be able to communicate in my own tongue ... there I go again! The struggle goes on but the Lord lays His hand on my shoulder and says, "As I was with Moses, so I have been with you, and will continue to be as long as you continue to trust me and obey."

When God answers, we may not like the answer, but He does answer and He is faithful.

Living Testimony Series from OMF

WHEN GOD GUIDES.

Denis Lane sets out ten principles for knowing God's guidance. Does God guide individuals? Is guidance confined to the big things of life or must I refer everything to His direction? In this book guidance is clothed in flesh and blood.

WHEN THE ROOF CAVES IN.

Sometimes we feel we are all alone in our agony. These testimonies reveal how people have coped with bereavement, accident, cot death, fire, sickness and separation. Missionaries for whom the roof has caved in bare their hearts and share some of their feelings and experiences. Denis Lane gives some pointers towards coping with such feelings, while veteran Bible teacher J Oswald Sanders brings biblical insights on the whole question of suffering.

WHEN GOD PROVIDES.

Dr James H Taylor spells out the principals by which the OMF has lived for the past 120 years and by which it still lives today. This is brought to life by over 70 testimonies covering topics which range from a second-hand tooth to a US$14,000 debt, from winter clothes in the right colours to the special need Asians have to give financial support to their parents.